Mixed Nuts

or What I've Learned Practicing Psychotherapy, ...in Plain English

By Rick Cormier

To TANDi FROM A NUT—

Copyright©2016 Rick Cormier

All Rights Reserved

First Printing

ISBN: 978-0-9974721-0-3

The Title

from *"My Life Cracks Me Up"*

I was working for a mental health agency in Massachusetts which hosted a reception for the mayor of the city. Clinicians were encouraged (required) to attend and meet the mayor.

My friend, Carl, was in line to shake hands with the mayor before me. Carl tended to be a real stiff – anal-retentive – detail-oriented to a fault. I don't know why such opposites as us got along so well, but we did.

Carl, standing in front of me in line and looking impeccable in his best suit, gave the mayor a firm handshake and said, "I'm Carl Stiff, licensed clinician for the Adult Outpatient Department, specializing in depression and anxiety, utilizing treatment modalities such as cognitive-behavioral and transpersonal models."

Only Carl could squeeze his resume into a handshake. I wanted to chuckle.

Instead, I shook the mayor's hand and grinned and said, simply,

"Rick Cormier. Mixed nuts."

TABLE OF CONTENTS

Foreword

Counseling and psychotherapy books are often written by professionals with teaching and research backgrounds whose clinical experiences are limited to their graduate school or internship placements of years ago. It is rare for someone such as Rick, who experienced depression as a teenager, to orchestrate his own recovery, get professional training in mental health, and then undertake a successful clinical practice utilizing his unique perspective. Now, upon his "semi-retirement," Rick has integrated his knowledge as well as his personal reflections and insights into this book and presented them in a way that should appeal to both professionals and the general public. Don't underestimate the mind and heart behind his playful humor and disarming smile.

Mental health service is enigmatic and often frustrating. Many interacting variables – biological, social, cultural, environmental, as well as the ecology of our body systems – affect the mind, including our unique existential and spiritual perspectives, and our own personal experience. One problem is that people who provide services, whether providing psychotropic medication or counseling and therapy, often operate within a rigid frame of knowledge and lack innovation and flexibility. When a particular client does not appear to respond to a given modality, the assumption is the client is not ready to respond or rejects recommendations he was offered rather than question the need for the mental health professional to adapt and/or innovate strategies to meet the client's needs.

This was where Rick excelled as a Psychology Department intern. Perhaps because he was older and more mature than other Doc torate and Masters level interns, perhaps because he had abandoned a lucrative career as a Human Resource executive to pursue one in mental health, or perhaps because he is an inherently creative individual, Rick approached each individual case as though he had discovered a new mental illness which required an innovative intervention. His patients benefited greatly.

I had the privilege to supervise Rick for nearly two years when he was interning at Taunton State Hospital. He also worked with me as group treatment co-facilitator for severely and persistently mentally ill clients, such as persons with schizophrenia, using elements of the Mind Stimulation Therapy model, then in the rudimentary phase of its development.

I was impressed then by Rick, as I am now, based on his current activities and his writings. Because of Rick's many other interests and his boundless energy, and, notwithstanding, having a supportive and understanding life partner in his wife, Judy, he decided to retire from clinical work to pursue other interests. But he has not lost his interest in sharing, caring, and helping others with his knowledge, insights, and skills. Rick has written a book that epitomizes and attests to this, that I am sure many will find useful and inspiring reading.

Mohiuddin Ahmed, Ph.D., Bellingham, Massachusetts

Consulting Clinical Psychologist in RI and Massachusetts: Active contributor to mental health journals and blogs, pioneered mind stimulation therapy, and co-authored Mind Stimulation Therapy: Cognitive Intervention for Persons with Schizophrenia

Opening Parable

(Author unknown)

An elephant lived at a zoo in a pen that was only 40' x 40' square. All day, the elephant would walk the 40 feet, turn and walk back.

The zookeeper was abusive. He would get drunk at night and stand on one side of the elephant's pen and hit the poor animal with a stick each time he reached that side of the pen. As a result, the elephant always winced when he reached that side of the pen, whether the zookeeper was there or not.

The zookeeper was eventually fired, and a new zookeeper was hired in his place. The new zookeeper was horrified when he saw the size of the elephant's pen. He ordered that a new 400' x 400' pen be built around the old pen, landscaped to reflect the elephant's natural habitat.

When the new pen was completed, the old fencing was removed. The zookeeper and the visitors were disappointed to see the elephant walk 40 feet, wince, then turn and walk back 40 feet in the opposite direction.

INTRODUCTION

So why did I just tell you a story about an elephant?

Because we're like that elephant*.

Many mental health problems begin with our attempts to cope with bad situations. We build emotional and behavioral defenses which become habits. Like that elephant, we carry imaginary fences in our minds and behave as if those fences were plain for everyone to see.

I don't even remember where I heard or read that story. I remember it struck me as profound because it occurred to me that my job as a psychotherapist was to get people to walk *41 feet,* just a step outside their comfort zone.

It's not enough to tell people that there is a world of choices open to them. Our "world" is whatever size we *perceive* it to be. Some of us need to see that we will survive taking that one extra step.

* *Also, because none of my previous books had any elephant stories and the elephants have been complaining.*

Long before I became a licensed mental health counselor, I suffered from depression as a teenager. I was prescribed all sorts of medications, none of which helped. At the age of 16, I bought a book of Gestalt Therapy exercises. Today, I would never recommend self-directed Gestalt Therapy as a treatment for depression, but I wasn't this smart at 16. I just knew my life had to change.

So I memorized the exercises and did them whenever I could. I even carried a scrap of paper in my pocket to remind me to do them.

Several years later, while sitting in a park reading Ralph Waldo Emerson, I had a "peak experience." Some might call it a "religious experience", or an "ecstatic experience." You can call it an "emotional and intellectual orgasm" for all I care.

I got it.

All the pieces fell into place.

Everything changed for me at that moment. There was a drastic shift in how I saw myself, others, and the differences between us. I went from the belief that I was a victim of my circumstance to the realization that I had choices and the responsibility for those choices. I went from the belief that everyone was in it for themselves to the realization that we all are connected. I understood for the first time that, if I had lived your life, I'd be more like you and vice versa. I understood that depression was a disease of thought, perception, and behavior, which meant that changing one's thought, perception, or behavior would change one's depression.

And I was right.

It's ironic that I went through my teens convinced I didn't "fit" in this world, that I would never make any meaningful contribution. But, since that day, life has never stopped surprising me.

Most people who know me as an adult have a hard time imagining me with depression. I'm the opposite of depression. I'm upbeat with a ready smile. I love to laugh and make jokes and tell funny stories. I like people a lot. I've met only a handful of people that I seriously disliked. I'm a chatterbox when talking about certain subjects. I can be high energy and intense, yet have no trouble relaxing. Even in semi-retirement, I divide my time moving from project to project. I've devoted most of my life and livelihood to doing things I enjoy that make even the smallest contribution to this nutty world.

No therapist is perfect for everyone. I tend to focus on a person's problem and its solution rather than chat week after week like a casual acquaintance in a laundromat. Clients who only wish to complain week after week and expect their therapist to simply lend a sympathetic ear and gently pat the top of their hand saying, "You poor, poor Dear. However do you manage?" are horrified by me. I'm okay with that. They're not my clientele. It will soon become apparent to the reader that I tend to be blunt, opinionated, and playful. I also care very much about my clients and work very hard to help them walk that one extra foot.

My favorite professor in grad school, John Twomey, EdD, once told our class, "If you can't lighten up and *play* with life, what do you imagine that you can teach people with mental health problems?" He encouraged us to relax and be ourselves during the therapeutic hour.

This made sense to me since, in the mental hospital where I served as an intern, my patients were either emotionally rigid or emotionally vacant. He also encouraged us to interact with clients as we would our peers.

So, from very early on, I worked at keeping my psychotherapy sessions as light and upbeat as possible. Throughout my career, my therapeutic goal was to make not only long-term gains but short-term gains. I wanted clients to walk out of my office feeling better than they did when they walked in. I gave myself extra points if they left smiling or chuckling.

My favorite clinical supervisor, Michael Meleedy, LICSW, once said to me, "I don't think that your success with anxiety clients is due only to all those techniques you use. I think it's *you*. I picture you sitting back in your chair listening to your clients with that huge grin of yours. You just rub off on people!"

I laughed at that, but I had to admit there was some truth to it, too. Part of my success with anxiety clients was that I was so relaxed and casual I drove them nuts!

I'll share a favorite example:

I was to meet Frau Striktbottom* at 4 o'clock for her initial intake appointment (diagnostic interview). My 3 o'clock client had her hand on the doorknob about to make her exit at 3:55 when she thought of one more thing she wanted to share. By 4 o'clock, she was in tears.

Now, I couldn't just say, "Your time is up. You have to go. I have another appointment." I listened and helped her regain enough composure so she could leave the office with some emotional stability. It was now about 4:10.

I went to the waiting room and saw this large, middle-aged, matronly woman. Imagine a refrigerator with arms, legs, and a head.

"Frau Striktbottom?"

"Are you Mr. Cormier?" she asked in a tone much like you would expect from the Queen of England asking why I had failed to remove the chamber pot from her room.

"Yeah, I'm Rick."

"Do you realize that we had an appointment for 4 PM, and it is now 4:13?" she asked while incessantly tapping the crown of her watch.

* Her name was not 'Frau Striktbottom'. I can't put clients' names in print, so I'll just assign people names that seem to fit.

"Is it? ...Huh! Are you ready?" I asked, smiling.

She followed me to my office, and we sat for an hour going through the agency's standard intake questions. She was a nice lady. She had been raised by people whose idea of parenting was filling her head with rules instead of filling her heart with love. At the end of the session, I said, "Your intake is finished. Now, I can set you up with a therapist who is older, younger, female, whatever, or I'd be happy to work with you if you like."

She looked me straight in the eye and said, "I wasn't one bit impressed with you when we met, but, after talking with you, I suspect there is something I could learn from you. If you don't mind, I think I would prefer to work with you."

Four months later, we said goodbye with heartfelt hugs. That Christmas season, she spotted me at an indoor mall, and we gave each other a last big hug.

So, yeah. Maybe I rub off on some people.

I decided some time ago that, if I were ever to write a book on mental health, it wouldn't be a technical and scholarly textbook with charts and statistics to prove the validity of my ramblings. There are thousands of books like that out there. They double as sleep-aids.

If I should sound callous when telling stories of past clients, I assure you I am not. In the course of doing my job, I have known several thousand clients on a very intimate and personal level. I have worked hard to help them. To avoid losing my own sense of self and risking burnout, I've learned to step back emotionally, once the work is done. When you step back, you begin to see the patterns and the humor.

My goal is to pass along what I have learned about mental health based on my experience as a clinician. (Your experience may differ.) I'll also share what I hope are some interesting stories.

My challenge is to communicate to you, the reader, in the same way that I would a client in the office, with plain language, an open heart, and with lightness and humor.

This book will not be encyclopedic in scope. You'll find no scholarly footnotes or bibliography. I'll speak from memory and often in generalities. There are no chapters on ADD, Bulimia, or Athlete's Foot. They're not my thing. I will talk about Anxiety, Trauma, Anger Management, Schizophrenia, Depression, and Relationships. I'll touch on anything insightful or entertaining that I think might be of interest.

Maybe I can even make you smile.

We could all stand to lighten up.

HOW DID I WIND UP HERE?

"When we are no longer able to change a situation - we are challenged to change ourselves." ~*Viktor E. Frankl*

After my journey through depression, I became fascinated with mental illness. I felt like I had successfully scaled a tall fence and reached the other side. I wondered if I could help others do the same. I was a huge fan of Gestalt Therapy and its founder, Fritz Perls, and saw myself as a Gestalt Therapist one day. I even had a huge poster of Fritz Perls in my bedroom. Fritz was bald with a serious-looking German face and a beard that began way above his ears and ended considerably below his chin. My friends thought it was a poster of Santa Claus.

After my first year of study at Southeastern Massachusetts University, I applied to Antioch West in San Francisco and was accepted with a full academic scholarship to their Psychology Masters Degree program. This meant six years of working with the psychology leaders of the 1970s at the Esalen Institute in Big Sur, California. Several months before I left for San Francisco, Antioch West was closed. "Thank you for your interest in Antioch West." I re-enrolled at Southeastern Massachusetts University.

SMU didn't have a great psychology department, so I changed my major to Communications. Maybe I could write for PBS someday. But months before I graduated, I thought I might enjoy working in Human Resources since, in my work-study job, I was often called on to handle employee relations issues. I was lucky enough to land a job in that field.

12 years later, I had worked my way up to a Director of Human Resources. I worked for the 60th largest company in the U.S. I earned a lot of money, and I was miserable. Working in Human Resources was fun at first. I loved identifying and hiring good people and putting them on a career path. I loved fighting to offer the best pay and benefits to retain good employees.

Then the political climate changed. Company loyalty toward employees was replaced by an obsession with the bottom line: profit above all else. The question of "How much pay and benefits should we offer to keep the best people?" was replaced with "How much pay and benefits can we take away before we lose our best people?" People who left were not replaced. Instead, the job responsibilities of the employees who remained were expanded. Their pay remained the same. People were now "cross-trained" to minimize the adverse effects of employees quitting. All of these cost savings were diverted upward in the form of CEO bonuses.

The fun went out of Human Resources. I recall one company Vice President, upon deciding to eliminate our head of Research and Development telling me, "I'll break the news. You clean up afterward."

Each year, our Sales Department was asked to project the sales for the coming year. They would arrive at a number – let's say 100 million dollars – and then they would slap each other's backs, hire a yacht, load it with food, liquor, and mistresses, and spend a weekend celebrating their fictitious number at company expense.

Near the end of that year, when it became apparent that our sales wouldn't even amount to 70% of the estimate, my job was to lay off hundreds of hourly employees who had successfully done the work they were paid to do. This was an attempt to minimize the theoretical loss caused by the exaggerated fictitious number. At the beginning of each year, the Sales Department made up another number, slapped each other's backs, hired their yacht, and the whole process began again.

Not that I'm bitter, mind you.

The line, "I hire people for a living." was replaced with "I lay people off for a living." I averaged two to three migraines per week. My company sent me to shut down entire facilities because I talked with each employee individually and no one had committed suicide or slashed executive tires or rampaged with firearms.

There was some multi-million dollar embezzling going on in my division of the company. Just as the parent company was about to fire the Vice President responsible, a less-reputable company made an offer to buy our division. At this point, my wife and I talked. My salary amounted to two-thirds of our joint income, and we had just become parents, but she wanted her husband back. It was time to walk away. I gave my notice and left. I received *two* severance packages. One to tell the new company everything I knew about the embezzling and the other from the former company to agree not to go public with what I knew.

My life cracks me up.

The statute of limitations has expired, and the division was sold and soon bankrupted (they didn't believe me about the embezzling), so I'm giving you the short version of a very long story.

Those severance packages funded grad school in Counseling Psychology. We complain when it doesn't, but sometimes life works out just fine.

The Journey Toward Licensing

After saying goodbye to Corporate America and deciding that psychotherapy was *still* what I would prefer to do for a living, I first had to apply to and be accepted by a grad school. A former undergrad professor and friend, Dr. Walter Cass, told me about a program in Cambridge, Massachusetts where one could cram 50 credits of academics, two years of internship, and the writing of one's thesis into a two-year program.

The program was called "Cambridge College." It was the brainchild of Eileen Moran Brown, Ph.D., who originated it in her Harvard University doctoral dissertation. When I attended, it was an adult education program that used Harvard's classrooms, professors, and library. Today, Cambridge College has its own building and professors.

When I opened the letter of acceptance, I paced around the house saying, "Oh, shit! Oh, shit! Oh, shit!" I had been out of college for 13 years. My ability to simulate study habits was ancient history.

What the hell was I thinking?

I had a friend who was seeing a pretty good therapist. He told his therapist that I was about to start the Cambridge College program, and it turned out that was where the therapist had studied. He offered to talk with me.

He gave me two great pieces of advice:

1) Do your internship in a mental hospital. You'll always know how severe a patient's illness is, since you'll be familiar with the furthest end of the spectrum, and everyone you'll treat afterward will seem easy, by contrast.

2) Work with every population and illness you can. You may find that you are particularly good or have fun working with a specific illness. Make that your specialty.

It proved to be valuable advice. While most of my classmates had easy internships working with the "worried well", only one female classmate and I opted for internships working with seriously mentally ill people.

I landed an internship with the Psychology Department of Taunton State Hospital in Taunton, Massachusetts. The orientation was memorable. The hospital administrator asked if I had ever noticed homeless people walking around waving their arms and ranting to no one in particular. Of course, I had. He said that we assume that those poor homeless souls are drunks and failures, but the hospital employees knew differently. These were mental hospital patients who were discharged and transferred to newly-funded group homes during the Reagan administration. Most patients were forced into group homes, after which more than 90% of all state mental hospitals were closed. Then, the new group homes were defunded and closed the following year.

He felt it was important that I understood that those rambling homeless people were mental patients who were thrown out of the health care system without medication or resources simply to save money. It happened to millions of mental patients across the country. Most lacked the ability to walk into a Social Security or welfare office and ask for help. I think about this every time I see a homeless person talking to no one in particular.

On my first day, I was given keys to the locked wards immediately after being given a tour of the hospital.

The first time I had to open one of the locked ward doors I was apprehensive. The big sign on the door read,

WARNING!
Risk of Escape

I turned the key in the lock, but the door wouldn't budge. There was only a small window at eye level. All I could see were beige corridor walls. I began to wonder if there were a bunch of lunatics crouched down on the other side of the door waiting to make a run for it. Would I be trampled in the process? What in the hell was I even doing here?

I pushed the door a little harder, and it moved a bit. There seemed to be something on the floor wedged against the door! As I pushed, the thin, frail body of an elderly woman wearing a flimsy hospital gown slid across the floor, unresponsive.

It would be my introduction to Irene Icicle.

Irene had catatonic schizophrenia. She would freeze like a statue at any moment for an indeterminate period. Irene had just curled herself up in front of the door and froze in place. None of the staff had spotted her yet. You can't imagine how weird it felt opening a big, heavy door while pushing a human being on the other side of it.

Apparently, Irene had been a promising 19-year-old student when one day, while entering a grocery store, she froze in the doorway. That happened more than 40 years before. Since then, she had stopped speaking and would freeze unpredictably. She spent her life in the hospital ever since.

Irene had what we call "flat affect". She was emotionless. Blank. The staff nurses moved her regularly from her bed to a chair and back. They spoon-fed her at mealtimes. It was sad to see a human being who was so vacant. I wondered what, if anything, was going through her mind. We would never know. My only consolation was the fact that catatonic schizophrenia is so rare.

My clinical supervisor was Dr. Mohiuddin Ahmed, who would later develop "Mind Stimulation Therapy." For the first several weeks I accompanied him when he talked with his patients. Then he and I would sit and talk afterward. I couldn't have asked for a better supervisor and mentor. Dr. Ahmed was always generous with his time and knowledge.

One day, during a Psychology Dept. meeting, the psychologists decided that I should be assigned to work with Manny Melancholia.

Manny was in his late 30s. Portuguese, Catholic, married with children – and gay. His Catholic faith and his Portuguese culture dictated that gay people were an abomination, so he denied his sexuality for as long as he could. Finally, he had taken a knife and stabbed himself in the stomach to end his misery.

He was going to be my first patient.

It didn't seem fair. I liked this guy. He was friendly, soft-spoken, easy to spend time with — and full of self-loathing. He deserved to have an experienced professional who could actually help him. I still had training wheels! If I failed, he might succeed in killing himself the next time...

(Oh shit...)

The only thing I could think to do was to convince him that being gay was okay, that it was normal, that his culture and religion were both mistaken. This coming from a straight married guy.

Life sometimes has a twisted sense of humor.

We talked and talked, about sexuality, religion, and cultural norms. In the end, he was released and never hospitalized again.

At this point, you may be wondering whether he went back to his wife and kids or joined a Barbra Streisand review on South Beach. The reality is, we don't get to hear what happens when patients are released unless they're hospitalized again.

After treating Manny, I was assigned to several other patients with depressive and bipolar diagnoses. Then I met my first schizophrenic patient.

When Dr. Ahmed introduced me to G.I. Joe, he said, "Don't try to do therapy with him." Then he left before I could ask what he meant. I later found out Dr. Ahmed only meant for me not to try to "cure" him.

If I wasn't supposed to do therapy, I guess I could just listen and keep our meeting conversational. As in art and music, sometimes accidents yield the best ideas.

Joe was a tall, thin, well-dressed guy in his late 20s. He seemed somewhat normal and sociable until he began telling me about how he fought in Vietnam at the age of six, later to be recruited by the CIA at age 13. Bizarre as this sounded, I just listened patiently. When he described something awful, I took it at face value and said, "That sounds really horrible!" He asked if we'd be working together on a weekly basis.

Dr. Ahmed was pleasantly surprised at Joe's response to me. Joe was reluctant to work with *anyone*. As soon as he was "redirected" (e.g., told that six-year-old kids weren't drafted to fight in Vietnam), he would shut down and refuse to talk with that person again. I just listened and didn't challenge his delusions.

Joe had bigger problems than these delusions. Joe would see a random man and his wife or girlfriend and get it into his head that the woman was *his* wife or girlfriend. He would figure the guy she was with must have kidnapped her and now has her against her will. Joe's mission was to rescue her from her kidnapper, so Joe would begin to plot against the guy.

Joe had been hospitalized in a locked ward for several years. His medication stopped him from forming new delusions. I helped him distinguish between likely memories and unlikely memories. He improved his social skills by regularly interacting with me. I became his mirror, letting him know when he sounded crazy. We even played guitars together outdoors one summer afternoon. He was released six months after we met.

The last time we saw one another was a few years later. I had pulled up to a gas pump on my motorcycle. Joe hopped out of his pickup truck and said Hi. He told me he had a job he enjoyed and had his own apartment.

For the rest of my mental hospital internship, working with paranoid schizophrenia became my "thing." I discovered that just listening established trust. When a patient trusted me and our relationship felt solid, I would look for one minor problem with which I could help. That small success would open the door to discussing their delusions and hallucinations in a way they could understand and accept. I also did my best to make them laugh and give them some semblance of personality and social skills. Mind you, little of this would have been possible without the help of anti-psychotic medication to curb the hallucinations and prevent the formation of new delusions.

I had to keep a serious face while listening to patients tell me that they could read minds, or that they worked for the FBI, the CIA, or God Himself, or that they owned 2002 different companies, wrote Star Wars, married John Kennedy and were in constant contact with the mother ship.

During my internship at the hospital, I treated only one patient who really scared me. Not only was Hannibal Wrecktor on a locked ward, but he was also locked in his *room*! This was quite unusual.

This was Hannibal's 42nd hospitalization. He suffered from severe Bipolar Disorder and enjoyed hitting people when he lost his temper. He was here because, while arguing with his 18-year-old daughter, he punched her so hard in the stomach that it had aborted her pregnancy. I was asked to meet with him to determine whether he was a good candidate for individual therapy.

One of the staff unlocked his door and told me to knock when I was ready to leave. I wondered how long it would be before someone heard me knock or scream.

Hannibal sat on his bed. He appeared middle-aged, disheveled, and sluggish, with one seriously mean-looking face. I offered my hand and said, "Hi! I'm Rick Cormier." Instead of shaking my hand, he looked at it as if it were a dead rat. I sat on the empty bed across from him.

"So, how are you?" I asked.

Hannibal just sat there staring at me. I wondered how long it would take for him to jump up from his bed and kill me.

"Do you think you might want to work with someone on a one-on-one basis?"

He just glared at me. I wondered how long it would take for me to get to the door and break it down with my fists.

"Well, Hannibal, it's been a pleasure meeting you!" I lied.

I went to his door and knocked. Thankfully, I soon heard the sweet sound of the door unlocking.

I headed back to Dr. Ahmed's office, with the intention of telling him that this guy was definitely not a candidate for individual therapy. Dr. Ahmed was busy on one of the wards. No problem. I'd tell him tomorrow.

That evening, I had a class in clinical work with Dr. John Twomey. I told him and the class about my experience with Hannibal. My classmates were horrified! Most of them treated clients who suffered from disorders such as Acute Disappointments, Chronic Dissatisfaction, and Unmet Expectation Disorder. The idea of treating actual crazy people was entirely foreign to most of them.

Dr. Twomey listened to my story and asked if I planned to see Hannibal again.

"No way! He's not ready for individual treatment!"

"I want you to do me a favor," he said. "See him just one more time. But, this time, don't feel pressured to draw him out. Say hi, but then just sit there and wait for him to talk. I promise you won't have to wait even 30 seconds before he says something."

I was torn between relief that I would never have to see Hannibal again and my admiration for Dr. Twomey, who was the most intuitive therapist I've ever known. He was known for making predictions like that in class, and he was always right. I so wanted to be as good as John Twomey.

So I agreed.

The door was unlocked, and I was led into Hannibal's lair once again. I said, "*Hi.*" and sat on the empty bed.

...and waited.

After about 20 seconds of awkward silence (though it seemed like much longer) Hannibal frowned and said, "So, how are *you* doing?"

Two weeks later, his door was unlocked for the last time. He and I began having our sessions while walking the hospital grounds twice a week. Thanks to the medication regimen and his new anger management skills, he was calm and stable enough to be released several months later. I have never been afraid of another patient or client since.

I received several nice bits of recognition during my hospital internship. The first was during a Psychology Department meeting when the psychologists were discussing a particularly challenging case of a schizophrenic woman, Wilma Wheels, who had nearly killed a stranger with her car, believing that he was out to kill her.

A woman in her residency to become a psychiatrist had refused to work with Wilma, stating that working with Wilma was "impossible." The Psychology staff was trying to decide who would provide individual psychotherapy when Dr. Ahmed suggested assigning her to me. One of the other psychologists in the meeting said, "If you assign her to Rick Cormier, she'll be out of here in six months!"

Interns didn't attend department meetings, but Dr. Ahmed was kind enough to pass that compliment along.

I became Wilma's therapist, and she was indeed a handful. The episode that brought her to the hospital happened when she came upon another car, driven by a stranger, ahead of her on the highway. She convinced herself that he was a member of the Mafia out to kill her because she worked for the FBI. (She once told me the FBI had installed a communication device in her chest so that they could communicate with her directly through her body.)

She knew she had to kill him before he could kill her. It's important to bear in mind that all the while she was driving *behind* him. The stranger didn't even know she existed. When he took his exit off the highway, she followed.

The poor guy pulled up to a pump at a gas station. Before he could step out of his car, Wilma rammed him from behind at full speed. Most of us in that situation would have chalked this up as a terrible accident. But imagine what went through his mind when he realized that the impact has caused his door to be jammed shut. When he looked in his rearview mirror, he saw Wilma about to ram him *again!*

She rammed him *six times* before anyone managed to stop her.

When police arrived, Wilma Wheels calmly explained that her husband was Carl Reiner, and they were filming a movie. "No need to worry, officer. It was all make-believe!"

Each time Wilma told me the story it changed. First, they were filming a movie. Next time, the story was that someone had put 25 LSD tablets in her Pepsi that morning. Then it was FBI vs. Mafia: kill or be killed.

This was unusual because most paranoid schizophrenics have one story that permeates their obsessive consciousness. Wilma had an endless supply.

I listened to them all.

When she began trusting me, and with the help of anti-psychotic medication, she and I worked well together.

I finished grad school about nine months later and got my first mental health agency job. They released Wilma from the hospital a few months after that. Her hospital treatment team knew I had been hired by a local mental health agency, so they set her up to see me weekly on an outpatient basis to help put her life back together. She was the only person I ever saw both as an inpatient and an outpatient. Wilma always asked how my toddler son was doing. She loved hearing little stories about him. I suspect that Wilma regretted being childless. She once bought him a Match-box car as a gift. Schizophrenics rarely give gifts.

A classmate once asked me how I could work with "crazy" people like schizophrenics. I said, " I don't work with crazy people. I work with the person trapped inside."

The other piece of recognition I received from the hospital was when they released G.I. Joe after his extended hospitalization. Dr. Ahmed asked me to do a presentation to staff psychiatrists, psychologists, and social workers, describing how I worked with Joe. This was unusual. Doctors don't fill a room to listen to interns. But I addressed a standing-room-only audience. Boy, was I nervous! I didn't relax until the question and answer period.

One of my funnier internship experiences happened one day when one of my patients who believed that he was God told me how he had created the oceans and the malls on the same day. Later that same afternoon, a female patient who believed that she was Jesus Christ told about how she invented water. I wondered if she knew that a guy on the men's ward was taking credit for it.

It was fun seeing God and Jesus on the same day. I hoped that, if anyone was admitted believing they were the "Holy Ghost," they would be assigned to me so that I could say I had treated the Trinity.

One of the interesting things I observed about paranoid schizophrenics is that a good number of them have delusions revolving around religious deities while another good number have delusions which revolve around government intelligence agencies (CIA, FBI, etc.) Religious authorities and government authorities.

Before wrapping up my internship experience, I should mention Uri Yakker.

I spotted Uri on my first day while getting the tour of the hospital. Uri had disorganized or hebephrenic schizophrenia. He stood against a wall in the hallway mumbling all day. As I got used to Uri's mumbling, I realized that he was talking very, very fast.

Weeks later, I got so accustomed to the sound of his mumbling, I began to hear the words: "I'll f_ck your mother, I'll f_ck your sister, I'll f_ck your father, I'll f_ck your brother, I'll f_ck your dog, I'll f_ck your cat, I'll f_ck the canary up the ass if it gets in my way."

Uri was *not* considered a candidate for psychotherapy.

He would never be my client. Still, I used to say hi to him whenever I passed him in the hall. He didn't respond.

Then, one day, during the second year of my internship, I said hi to Uri, and he looked straight at me for the first time and said, "One for the money!"

I was shocked! I stopped and replied, "Two for the show."

Uri: "Three to get ready."

Rick: "Four to go."

Uri: "Five's alive."

Now, like a man with no legs, I was stumped. I had never heard this little rhyme go beyond the number four.

Uri pointed to me, indicating that it was my turn and said, "Six to do tricks."

Then he pointed to himself. "Seven go to heaven."

He taught me the whole routine, right up to ten. During my second year at the hospital, every time I said hi to Uri he responded with "One for the money." and we went through our routine.

On my last day at the hospital, which Uri could not have possibly known, he looked right at me and said, quite lucidly, "You always talk to me like a person. One for the money!",

and we went through our routine one last time.

~:~:~:~:~

Grad school was a surprise. I had no idea I'd be given a week to read four books at a time. No one warned me that I would be required to write 10- to 25-page papers plus a two-page paper for each class while simultaneously working on my master's thesis. For nearly two years. I saw my wife and son mostly on weekends.

I had decided in grad school that the best way to be good at psychotherapy was to have lots of techniques up my sleeve to increase my chances of reaching the most people and treating the most disorders.

For instance, cognitive therapy is considered the treatment of choice for depression but, the fact is, cognitive therapy works best for people who spend lots of time up in their head thinking. It's not effective for treating everything and everyone. The whole "art" of doing therapy is being able to match the right treatment to both the problem and the patient/client.

There is behavioral therapy, interpersonal therapy, motivational therapy, brief therapy, hypnotherapy, Gestalt therapy, EMDR, TFT, VKD and much more. For therapists, these are the paints on our palettes. The more colors of paint on our palettes, the more people and illnesses we can treat.

Some students and practicing therapists make the mistake of mastering only one discipline. Then, they blame the client if it doesn't work.

Rogerian Therapy, also known as "Client-Centered Therapy," is common because it's easy to learn and requires the least effort and personal involvement on the part of the therapist. Rogerian Therapy is:

"What do YOU think is the answer to your question?"

and

"How did that make you feel?"

I've been known to promise clients that I would never ask how anything made them feel.

I don't care how you feel.
I care how you function.

My job is to help clients regain their functioning, to get them to walk 41 feet, then 42.

Dr. Jeffrey Arbetter was my other favorite grad school professor. He was the undisputed master of clinical techniques. He taught Rogerian Therapy, Cognitive-Behavioral, Rational Emotive Therapy, Hypnotherapy, and many others.

I had always wanted to be hypnotized. When stage hypnotists had audiences clasp their hands with fingers intertwined and said we couldn't pull our hands apart, no one was more disappointed to be able to pull his hands apart easily than I was.

So, when Dr. Arbetter asked for volunteers at the start of our class in Ericksonian Hypnotherapy, my hand shot up fast enough to catch a housefly in mid-air. He chose six of us to sit with him in a small circle while the rest of the class formed an outer circle and observed.

I expected Dr. Arbetter to tell us we were getting sleepy, but he just lectured from his place in our circle. I remember feeling the need to relax. I stretched out in my chair while still listening to him talk. Sometime soon after, I remember feeling that it would be good just to shut my eyes for a second. I could still listen.

It's important to point out the Dr. Arbetter was only talking about Milton Erickson. He never told us to relax or close our eyes. But all six of us had.

As it turned out, Dr. Arbetter was using the cadence of his speech coupled with synchronizing his breathing and eye blinking with each of us as he spoke. That was how he put us all in a trance. Even a few of the students observing us wound up hypnotized!

At one point during the hypnosis, Dr. Arbetter gave us the option of supplying our own post-hypnotic suggestion or getting one from him. I chose my own. When the session was over, a fellow student and I were talking about how powerful the experience was. The student was in mid-sentence when he suddenly collapsed in his chair like a wet piece of rope! I thought he had a heart attack or stroke and died!

It turned out he was the only one of us who took Dr. Arbetter's post-hypnotic suggestion. The suggestion was when Dr. Arbetter removed his glasses; the student would fall as deeply into trance as he was at that moment. I nearly had a heart attack at the sight of him collapsing in mid-sentence!

I was hooked. I read everything on Milton Erickson that I could. I even signed up to study Ericksonian Hypnotherapy through Harvard Medical School. I was probably the only student in that class who was *not* studying to be a physician.

It proved to be the best and most memorable class I ever took.

I recall that in one particular class, Dr. Brown, the professor, was talking about the importance of not asking "leading" questions during hypnosis because the unconscious mind will randomly make up any answers it doesn't know.

To illustrate his point, he asked for a volunteer. A female medical student raised her hand. Dr. Brown had her sit in the front of the room, facing us, and put her into a trance.

Dr. Brown: "What is my name?"

Hypnotized Student: "Doctor Brown."

Dr. Brown: "And where do I work?"

Hypnotized Student: "Harvard Medical School."

Dr. Brown: "And where do I live?"

Hypnotized Student: "In Arlington."

Dr. Brown: "What kind of car do I drive?"

Hypnotized Student: "A Porsche."

Dr. Brown: "What is my wife's name?"

Hypnotized Student: "Gail."

At this point, Dr. Brown looked up at the class, most of whom sat with bulging eyes and open mouths. (There were some pretty goofy people in our class, huh?)

Dr. Brown: "Did you think she was giving me the right answers? How could she possibly know the answers to those questions? What the unconscious mind doesn't know, it makes up! What do you suppose would happen if I asked her my social security number?"

Brown-Nosed Medical Student In Front Row: "She would make one up?"

Dr. Brown: "Of course! She doesn't know anything personal about me."

New-Agey Student Who Probably Owned More Than One Book On Aromatherapy: "What about past life regression? How does that work?"

Dr. Brown: "You believe in past life regression? Well, let's see. If I were to ask our subject here to go back to the time before she was born and then tell me what her name used to be, what would she do"?

Brown-Nosed Medical Student In Front Row: "She'd make up a name!"

Dr. Brown: "And if I asked her where she lived, what she did, who her friends were?"

Random Student: "She'd fabricate all those details."

Dr. Brown: "It works the same with dreaming, also. Our unconscious mind creates our dreams. The specific elements of our dreams – the people, places, and situations – are completely random. Only the emotions they evoke in us have any relevance."

All this took place during one single, unforgettable class!

That last point about dreams has served me well over the years. You would be surprised how many therapy clients expect us to interpret their dreams.

Milton Erickson became my hero, my ideal therapist. He could put someone in a trance wordlessly while shaking their hand. He was famous for "curing" patients in a single visit by determining what they needed and slipping the right suggestion into their subconscious while their defenses were down.

~:~:~:~:~:~

One of my pivotal grad school moments was when Dr. Twomey brought a mental patient to our class to talk about his illness. The guy introduced himself and described his family and his extremely abusive childhood in detail. When he finished his talk, Dr. Twomey thanked him for coming, and we all applauded.

After a break, Dr. Twomey pointed to a person in the front row and asked, "Diagnosis?" The student replied, "PTSD." "Based on what?" asked Dr. Twomey. The student went on to explain how anyone raised in such an abusive environment would be adversely affected.

Dr. Twomey wrote "PTSD" on the blackboard in big letters then pointed to the next student. "Diagnosis?"

"PTSD." was the reply. In fact, eight of the ten students in the clinical class agreed the man suffered from PTSD.

Then it was my turn. I took a long, deep breath.

"Paranoid Schizophrenia" I ventured.

"Paranoid Schizophrenia? Are you saying he was *lying?*"

Half the class glared at me while he wrote "Paranoid Schizophrenia" on the board.

"No" I replied. "I think he believes; I think he *remembers* exactly what he said. I just don't believe that it happened."

"Based on what?"

"Why would his parents single out only one child out of seven to torture like that? And also, he *feels* like one of my schizophrenic clients. Something I can't put my finger on."

"So, you think he's lying." Dr. Twomey wasn't making this easy.

I felt like crap!

He pointed at the last student. "Diagnosis?"

That student looked at me then back at Dr. Twomey. Reluctantly, she said "PTSD."

Dr. Twomey went to the blackboard and circled the words "paranoid schizophrenia" many times. Then he turned to me and smiled. The remainder of the class was devoted to talking about paranoid schizophrenia. I was happier than a fly in an outhouse!

A particularly embarrassing moment occurred when a professor psychoanalyzed me in front of the whole class. It began with our Relationship Counseling professor asking which domestic chores we didn't mind doing: washing dishes, ironing clothes, doing laundry, cleaning bathrooms or dusting.

Everyone named some tasks they didn't mind except me. I said I wouldn't want to do *any* of those. Many of the women in the class huffed and puffed and made faces as if someone had farted! The female professor calmed the women down and asked, "What's wrong?"

One woman in the class said, "What a chauvinist!" Our professor asked, "Based on his response, how many of you think that Rick is a chauvinist?"

Most of the female hands went up.

<sigh>

"Okay, let's see," said the professor. "Rick, stand up, please. Would you be willing to answer a few questions?"

"Sure," I said, pretending I didn't mind.

She went on to ask me a bunch of questions about my mother, and then questions about my father, all of which I answered.

Then she addressed the class. "You think this guy is a chauvinist? This guy is a *dream!* This guy loves women so much he became his father's opposite because he didn't like the cold, detached way his father treated his mother. You know *why* he doesn't want to wash dishes or clean bathrooms? Because he associates *any* mundane task with his father! Rick sees house cleaning the same way he sees his father's factory work. Did you hear him say he *cooks*? He described his mother as a "gourmet cook." What's the difference between cooking and doing laundry? Cooking is *creative*. He associates creativity with his mother! Give him a creative task, or any task that's non-routine, and watch him run with it!"

I have to admit, her summary was correct. I never saw myself that way, but even my wife admitted that it fit. It was just embarrassing to be singled out and analyzed in front of the class.

"Can I sit down now?"

~:~:~:~:~:~

My original plan was to intern at the mental hospital for one year and then find an outpatient setting to intern for my second year, but I was so involved with my work at the hospital that I decided to stay and add an outpatient internship in my second year. It meant I would be graduating with 50 percent more internship hours than the requirement for licensure, but my goal was to be damned good at what I did, not just meet the minimum requirements.

In my second year, I added an outpatient internship with the Veterans Administration, specifically, the Veterans Readjustment Counseling Service, AKA the "Vet Center." It was there I first learned to treat substance abuse and Post-Traumatic Stress Disorder (PTSD). I loved that year working with veterans.

Although I had studied hypnotherapy at Harvard Medical School, the VA's official position was that hypnosis was disallowed. They weren't as forward-thinking as they would later become.

My supervisor, Neil, was a pretty cool guy. He was a former Marine Sergeant, who always had small decorative fountains in his office. My most vivid memory of Neil's office is the constant sound of trickling water. I joked that his clients needed to pee more often than most.

Neil was also a hypnosis trainer. When I asked him about the VA's restriction on hypnosis, he smiled and said, "Do what you can to help your veterans. If you use any form of hypnosis, your clinical note should read that you did a 'guided visualization'" I was lucky to work with Neil.

Sometimes a veteran would prefer to have Neil as his therapist because he had been a Sergeant in the Marines and I was never a combat veteran. Neil would tell them, "If your issue were substance abuse, I'd be your guy. But for PTSD, Rick or Joan (the other full-time clinician in our office) will get you better faster than I will."

During that time, I was getting involved in community drum circles. I noticed a healing component to the group drumming. Depressed drum circle participants seemed less depressed. Shy, anxious participants became more relaxed and outgoing. It occurred to me that something more than musical recreation was going on. My theory was that this was happening because, to drum and listen at the same time, one had to shut off all the chatter in one's head for a few hours. Group drumming was an exercise in "mindfulness" before the word became popularized.

What if this could help our PTSD veterans?

I went to Neil, armed with every counter-argument I might need. I told him my idea and waited for his objections. "A drum circle for veterans sounds great!" said Neil. "When do you want to start? I can recommend some of my veterans, and I'm sure that Joan will want some of hers to participate."

That was Neil.

I ran that drum circle successfully for a few months. Some of those veterans got more symptom relief from the drum circle than they did from a year's worth of individual therapy. One 80-year-old WWII veteran was so enthusiastic about group drumming that his wife bought him a pair of bongos for Christmas!

When Neil's regional manager heard about my drum circle, she ended it. She didn't believe there was anything remotely therapeutic about group drumming. "If Rick Cormier were into playing cards he'd have our veterans all sitting around playing cards!" A bunch of the veterans approached me and offered to start a petition to keep the drum circle. I asked them not to. One veteran came to my office and said, "You can't give me something like drumming and then take it away. You have no idea how much this means to me, how much this is helping me!"

I told him about the community drum circle I ran downtown and said that, if he should ever show up, it was up to him whether to tell anyone that I was his therapist. Whether or not he said he knew me at all didn't matter. He became a regular. He and I even did a presentation, several years later, for the PTSD ward of a Massachusetts VA hospital and even had the doctors and nurses drumming with the patients!

One of the ironies of Neil's manager shutting down my drum circle was that, in the years that followed, clinicians from Vet Centers all over the country found my mention of drum circles for combat veterans on my drum circle's website and began emailing me asking how they should go about setting up drum circles for veterans with PTSD.

The most interesting and memorable fact I learned from Neil was regarding alcohol abuse. One day we were talking together in his office, and Neil said, "Well, the alcoholics drink more than 90% of the liquor produced in this country."

"What?? You made that up!" I countered.

Neil: "You don't believe me?"

Rick: "If only 22% of the public are alcoholics, how can they be drinking more than 90% of the liquor?"

Neil: "You consider yourself a social drinker, right? How many ounces of pure alcohol would you say you drink in a month?"

Rick: "Well, a 12-ounce beer contains about one ounce of alcohol, a 5-ounce glass of wine has one ounce, and hard liquor is ounce for ounce so I'd guess I'd average about 4 ounces of alcohol in a month."

Neil: "So you drink about 48 ounces of pure alcohol in a year. Before I got sober, when I was actively drinking in the Marines, I drank a fifth of whiskey every day. That's 25 ounces."

He let that sink in before continuing.

"That means that I drank more alcohol in *two days* than you do in a *year!*"

Lesson learned.

Time to Go to Work

After graduation, I began looking for a job with a community mental health agency. I got two offers. One with an agency in Taunton, Massachusetts, 30 minutes from home and one from an agency in New Bedford, Massachusetts, mere miles across the bridge. The New Bedford firm offered me a dollar more per hour. The choice would seem like a no-brainer.

But, the agency in Taunton had a pleasant receptionist and clinicians who, between clients, amiably chatted with one another. The atmosphere was friendly and relaxed. Even clients in the waiting room said hello.

The New Bedford agency had a receptionist who made me wait five minutes before she even lifted her head to ask what I wanted. The clinicians and staff there all looked frazzled and exhausted. The atmosphere was cold, impersonal, and rushed, like an Alaskan brothel on Nickel Night.

During my interview, the Director of the New Bedford agency told me that the staff went out to a local bar on Thursday nights. He asked if that would be a problem.

(Why would that be a *problem*? Why would I care what they do after work?)

"It's important that whoever we hire fits in with the rest of the staff."

(Is he saying that going out drinking with the staff on Thursday nights is a *job requirement?* I'm married to a woman with whom I enjoy hanging out. We have a baby. My teen years are behind me. Why would I want to go out and get wasted with co-workers on Thursday nights?)

I took the position in Taunton, 30 minutes away, for a dollar less per hour and never regretted it.

The first month with my new agency would set the course of my entire career.

First, the back-story.

Once, when I was in grad school, a male member of our class came in excited about a workshop he had just taken on the subject of treating sexual trauma victims. One of the women in the class said that a female sexual trauma victim would never see a male therapist. Half of the women in our class agreed.

I felt sorry for this poor guy. He shelled out $600 for a workshop he enjoyed, and now some women were hosing him down relentlessly. They started polling for other opinions. Some of the women bravely answered that it would depend on the male therapist. When they asked me, I replied, "I can't imagine a rape victim ever coming to me for therapy, so I don't have an opinion either way."

Life has a way of humbling us all.

During the first few weeks at my agency, I did an intake interview (the initial diagnostic meeting) with a woman who had been a victim of rape. After spending 90 minutes getting all her pertinent information as gently and sensitively as I could, I thanked her and announced that her intake was complete.

One of the things I've always done at the end of an initial meeting was to ask the client whether he or she was comfortable with me, or if they would prefer someone older, younger, female, gay, etc. It's a valuable tool because you either get a commitment from the client, or you make it easy for them to opt-out if they don't feel that you're a good fit.

That practice began in this particular interview. I said, "Your intake is complete. I have all the information I need. Now, I can set you up with a female clinician, if you'd like, or someone older or younger..."

She looked disappointed and said, "Oh. I thought that *you* would be my therapist."

"I'd be happy to work with you if you'd like," I said, pretending not to be flabbergasted.

"Yeah. You seem nice, and you're easy to talk with."

I set her up with an appointment for the following week. Then I went home and told my wife, "I've got a rape victim for a client! I have a week to become an expert in treating *rape!*"

I spent my evening hours researching from the psychology books I had accumulated. Of course, I was to learn that treating sexual trauma wasn't much different than treating combat veterans.

You just use less profanity when you talk.

When you speak with combat veterans with PTSD day after day, the conversation can sound like this:

Veteran: "So the fuckin' commander tells me to climb the fuckin' hill to see if I spot any of the fuckin' enemy!"

Me: "Shit! So what the fuck did you *do?!*"

As a male therapist, you can't talk with female rape victims like that. You must be able to draw from a softer, gentler side of your personality.

The reverse is also true. If you speak with a combat veteran with PTSD as gently and sensitively as you would a rape victim, you may wind up going out the fuckin' window!

PTSD was to become one of my two "specialties." Anxiety Disorders would be the other. That first rape client would be the first of scores of rape victims and incest survivors that I would work with over the course of my career.

During that same first month, I did an intake with a lesbian with relationship problems. Her partner was unwilling to join her for counseling. This woman was trying to fix their relationship on her own.

Same story: "Would you prefer to work with someone gay?"

"I can't work with *you?*"

There would never be a time in my career when I wasn't working with at least one gay person, male or female. The mentor who gave me such good advice before grad school was gay and had "*Gay Issues*" printed on his business card. I would tease him in subsequent years by reminding him that I saw more gay clients than *he* did!

After my first year with the agency, I got a call from Neil at the Vet Center. There was a part-time opening, and it was decided unanimously by both clinicians and the office manager that I should fill it. I worked full-time for my agency. I didn't need a 10-hour per week part-time job, but I jumped at the chance to work with veterans again.

One of the most unusual cases I worked with was Frank Fogg. Frank was a Vietnam vet in his 50s, average height, curly hair, slightly chunky build. His mental illness, paranoia, and short-term memory loss was the result of a head injury in Vietnam.

Frank always had about three inches of notepad pages bulging out of his breast pocket. These pages were filled with personal reminders. I accompanied him to the nearby pharmacy once and saw him file through what might have been nearly a hundred notes, to look up what brand of cigarettes he smoked. Then, he needed to go through them again to see what kind of chewing gum he liked.

Frank was a handful. Both Neil and Joan had worked with him in the past. Frank's short-term memory loss was so severe that, after years of coming to the Vet Center weekly, he still called to ask the Vet Center's address before each appointment.

What was worse was that Frank would forget details like how much money he had in the bank. He would see his balance and remember having had more in his account. Frank periodically insisted that his therapist brought him to the bank where he would accuse some poor bank VP of siphoning off his money. Of course, when they showed Frank the record of withdrawals he didn't recall, he convinced himself that the bank had falsified his records.

I listened to this sort of thing every week. Frank believed that his neighbors broke into his apartment while he slept and stole a can of tuna fish because he knew he bought three cans and not just two, and a 20-year-old pair of pants. ("If I had thrown them out I would have remembered, wouldn't I?")

Frank sat by his door at night with a baseball bat, ready to nail the imagined "son-of-a-bitch" who was stealing his stuff. Of course, he would eventually fall asleep. ("That's when the sons-of-bitches break in! As soon as I'm sleeping!")

Frank's VA Hospital psychiatrist wasn't treating him for paranoia. In fact, he had no idea that Frank was paranoid. Every few months, Frank would make the trip to the VA Hospital in Providence, Rhode Island and spend several hours in the over-crowded waiting room. When he finally got to see his psychiatrist, he was asked, "How are you doing?" Frank answered. "Fine", and the psychiatrist renewed his prescription. I asked Frank to tell his doctor about how he sat by his door with his baseball bat each night, but, of course, Frank forgot what I said within minutes! To make matters worse, his psychiatrist never returned my calls or answered my detailed letter.

Doing therapy with Frank was frustrating. We would have a breakthrough — Frank would gain insight — and 20 minutes later he couldn't even remember the conversation. Still, he denied having a memory problem.

Then one day, at the start of our session, I handed Frank my pack of cigarettes and asked him to count how many cigarettes were in my pack. He counted six. I asked Frank to write this down on a piece of paper and sign it. Then I put the paper and my cigarettes in an envelope and had him sign and seal it. I tucked it in my drawer, and we had our usual session.

Toward the end of the hour, I asked Frank if he remembered how many cigarettes had been in my pack. He had no idea why I was asking that question. I handed him the envelope and asked him to open it. He sat there staring at his note and the cigarettes, dumb-founded.

I told him about his memory problem. I asked him to write what happened on the back of the paper and then sign it again. I said that, from that day forward, anytime he was upset about someone "stealing" his cigarettes, or canned goods, or medication, or his 20-year-old pants, I was going to show him that piece of paper to remind him that he had a memory problem. It didn't solve his memory problem, but it helped move the therapy along because now we could address his memory loss.

A similar case involving short-term memory loss was Harry Callahan, whose third and final suicide attempt involved putting a revolver in his mouth and pulling the trigger. Not something you'd mistake as a "cry for help." Harry wanted to be out of here.

The bullet sailed through his palate, sinuses, and frontal lobe and exited, leaving Harry with not only short-term memory loss but with a hair-trigger temper that surfaced at random times. We would be chatting casually about anything, and Harry would get this bizarre look on his face and lunge from his chair wrapping both hands around my neck to strangle me. Tempted as I was to squeak, "Does somebody need a hug?", I would talk to him in a very soft voice, so he had to strain to hear me. That always snapped him out of it.

Once I had to transport him from New Bedford to Hyannis for an interview. It was about an hour's drive. That made me nervous. If he "snapped" and started strangling me while I was driving a government vehicle at highway speed it could have been disastrous.

He didn't. We had a friendly conversation the whole trip, and I even lived long enough to tell you the story.

~:~:~:~:~

I've often wondered why anxiety disorders became my other specialty. Why is it the one mental illness category that I have *fun* treating?

Is it because I use behavioral techniques that are most effective for treating anxiety? Is it, as Michael Meleedy implied, that I'm so relaxed and casual that I just "rub off" on my anxiety clients? Or is it that most anxiety clients are obsessive personality types (controllers), and I just have fun messing with them?

Perhaps a bit of all three.

One memorable moment from my early years in community mental health occurred during an initial session with a 60-year-old Italian woman named Isabella Fussolini, whose control issues were alienating her family.

At one point, I said to Isabella, "I would imagine that, if I saw your house right now, the bed would be made; the chairs are pushed in under the table; there are no dirty dishes in the sink;

the shower door is closed; the caps are on the hairspray can and the toothpaste tube..."

She said, "You think I'm like that? I'm not like that!"

"It was just a guess," I replied. Then I asked her a question. But, before she could answer, I took a tissue out of my tissue box, crumpled it up in my hand and tossed in on the floor between us.

As I expected, Isabella tried to answer my question but was distracted by the tissue. She could hardly take her eyes off it and was having real trouble concentrating enough to answer my question. Finally, she picked up the tissue, put it on my desk and answered the question.

I asked another question and before she could answer, dropped the tissue back on the floor. I smiled and said, "I *wanted* that there."

She tried to answer my question but was distracted again and reached down and picked up the tissue. As her head was coming up, she looked at me and said, "*You son-of-a-bitch!* Okay. The bed is made. The shower door is closed. I would *die* before I left my house with dirty dishes in the sink! The caps are on the hairspray and toothpaste..."

We worked successfully together for the next six months. Her family couldn't believe how much she changed. I got a Christmas card from her every year until I left Massachusetts.

This completely improvised incident marked the birth of the deviously playful persona that most of my anxiety clients would know.

I had six pictures on the office wall behind me, arranged in an asymmetric pattern that bothered obsessive types. I could even reach the picture behind me and make it crooked without looking at it. I would suggest that clients deal with it for the remainder of the session and have a good chuckle at themselves if it bothered them.

Even my state license to practice hung on a nail that caused it to be ever-so-slightly askew. When clients tried to straighten it, it fell right back ever-so-slightly where I wanted it. I drove obsessive clients nuts.

~:~:~:~

I was always more effective working with sexual abuse victims than with perpetrators. So, when I did an intake on a perpetrator, I pretty much knew in advance that I would not be his therapist.

There was an exception to this.

Chris Creepo was 20 years old when I met him. When he came into my office, he immediately pulled his chair away from the wall and so close to me that our knees were touching!

(WTF?)

I smiled and said, "This is *my* desk. Only I get to sit here. You get to sit over *there*."

It took him a few seconds to catch my meaning but then he abruptly apologized and moved his chair back to where it was.

Chris's mother had realized that she was a lesbian and threw Chris's father out of the house when Chris was a year old. Her lover moved in shortly after that. There was a lot of animosity on the part of the lover who apparently competed for Chris's mother's affection which had come to a head some months ago when the lover gave the ultimatum, "Him or me!" The mother chose her lover, and Chris went to a homeless shelter.

This was not Chris's complaint. What concerned Chris was how he spent his afternoons at the mall.

Chris would see a woman whose looks he liked. He would follow her around the mall, sometimes for hours. All this time he was working himself up sexually in his imagination. He would maneuver himself so that he would be walking down one end of an aisle when his 'target' was walking toward him. He would time it so that he passed her at the exact location of a pole or display so that he would have an excuse to brush up against her. He would be so worked up by then, he would have an orgasm right at that moment, just before he said, "Excuse me." The woman would have no idea this had just happened, and Chris Creepo would be on his way to the men's room to clean up.

YUCK!!

I was shocked! I'd never heard of such a thing. It turns out it was common enough to deserve a name. It's called "frotteurism." Since I didn't work with sexual deviates, Chris would be someone else's challenge.

The following week, Chris came in to complete the second half of the intake process. The first thing I noticed was that he didn't move his chair close to mine. It occurred to me that Chris essentially lacked a sense of boundaries. I had taught him something very basic about boundaries, and he had *learned it.* Could it be that simple?

Chris had grown up without a male influence. He had never worked at a job or driven a car. He had never had a girlfriend, and no one had ever sat down with him and talked about sex. All of his exposure to sex was through pornography. I discussed the case with Michael, my supervisor, who felt that what Chris needed might be just some basic re-parenting and that I just might be the guy to reach him.

Sure enough, soon after starting to work with me, Chris started modeling himself after me. He was an odd-looking young man. His hair had an overgrown spiked look, like a field of wheat overdue to be harvested. He picked up his knees more than necessary when he walked and always walked with his arms bent at the elbows. This gave him the overall appearance of wading through a waist-high swamp.

One day he came into my office all excited. "Notice anything different?!" he asked. I admitted I didn't.

"I'm wearing a button-down shirt like *you* wear! Even your favorite color: purple!"

Ho boy. Here was my twin.

Chris hoped someday to have a wife like mine, live in a house like mine, and drive a car like mine. Eventually, he would even start to rebel as he entered his emotional teen years.

On the other hand, Chris stopped stalking women at the mall. I taught him to make friends with girls, how to behave appropriately.

It's important to understand that this was a guy who once told me, "I'm nervous about having sex someday. I know from movies that you're supposed to cum in the woman's face, but I'm not sure that I'll be comfortable doing that." This is the kind of thing you learn when your only sex education is pornography. You'd probably also learn that every man has a 12-inch penis, but you.

Chris once asked me why you had to wait until a woman was having her period to have sex.

<Groan>

Chris's revealed that one of his favorite pastimes was pretending to be a 13-year-old girl in Internet chat rooms so that he could converse with young teen girls about sex. We stopped *that* practice in a hurry.

It's important to remember that Chris came to therapy *voluntarily*. He was not an evil guy. He was not court-ordered into treatment. Chris was the result of a young man's sexuality kicking in when there was no one to talk with about it. Misguided as he was, he *wanted* to be better.

I used to stress to Chris that I didn't want him asking a woman out on a date until I said he was ready. Let's work on friendships first.

One day he really goofed. He met a woman at a bus stop that he liked. They talked, and the conversation must have been appropriate because, when he asked her to have coffee with him sometime, she agreed.

And then he said, "I should warn you, though: my doctor has me on Prozac, and it makes it tough for me to get an erection or have an orgasm."

"You said WHAT???"

At least, his creepy behaviors had stopped. Chris left the homeless shelter and got his own apartment and had learned a lot about relationships by the time I left that agency. And it all started when I made a crack about respecting my personal space.

WHO'S AFRAID OF ANXIETY?

My Train Trestle Story

Sigmund Freud was said to have a 7% success rate working with anxiety disorders. That works out to a 93% failure rate. Why? Because he believed that the key to all mental illness was delving into a patient's past and finding its origin. In the case of anxiety disorders, the cure isn't there. Knowing the source of your emotional disorder doesn't cause it to disappear miraculously.

I'll tell my own story to illustrate the point.

I was about 16 years old, walking with three other friends along some local railroad tracks. Two friends were walking ahead engaged in conversation while Ray and I walked about 25 feet behind.

Ray was in mid-sentence when we reached a railroad trestle. I'm not talking about some ridiculously high movie trestle towering hundreds of feet above a raging river. I'm talking about the type of train trestle that towers about 12 feet above a city street. As soon as I attempted to step forward onto the trestle, my foot stopped.

I couldn't do it.

Now, even at the age of 16 I had size 12 feet. The spaces between the railroad ties on that trestle were no more than four inches apart. I couldn't squeeze my foot through a four-inch hole if my life depended on it. Yet, all I could feel was that my whole body would fall through if I stepped onto that trestle!

By now, poor Ray was nearly halfway across and still talking with me. At some point, he turned and saw that I was about 20 feet behind him trying to step onto the trestle. To make matters worse, when he reached the other side he bent down and grabbed hold of the train tracks and pretended to shake them.

<Sigh>

I couldn't do it! I couldn't walk across that trestle! I went around the long way and met my friends later.

It bugged me for weeks. I couldn't understand my reaction. I had grown up around those railroad tracks. Granted, we had moved from that neighborhood before I was ten, but why should crossing that trestle bother me? After some weeks, I had a vague recollection of a dream where I lost my shoe through a hole in a trestle. My brother climbed down to the street to get it for me. The next time I saw my brother, I told him the story.

"That wasn't a dream. That actually happened." said my brother.

"We were walking along the tracks. You were about five or six. I was 15 or 16. Your shoe got caught in a hole on the trestle and fell into the street below. They were new shoes, and I didn't want to get in trouble, so I climbed down to the street to get it before a car could run over it. I left you up on the trestle. No train was coming, but you got scared and cried until I got back."

It was even the same trestle!

That explained everything. A childhood trauma had left me with a phobia of train trestles. I couldn't walk on that trestle because of losing a shoe and being left alone up there when I was a little kid.

If Freud had been right, I'd have been cured. Knowing the origin of the phobia would have been enough to vanquish it.

It wasn't. It never is.

I took my bicycle back to the same spot and still couldn't do it. But I kept trying. I rode my bike to that trestle two or three times a week. I'd take a single step, then another, then another, then rush back. Eventually, step by step, I made it all the way across, about 40 feet. Then, of course, I was forced to walk the length of it again to get back to my bicycle.

Sounds a bit like the elephant story, doesn't it?

Today, I can walk across train trestles. I've even crossed some big ones — the movie kind that towers hundreds of feet above a raging river. I won't beat you in a race, but I'll get across just fine, not because I understand the origin of my fear, but because I did the tougher work of confronting it. I got my functioning back. I don't *enjoy* crossing trestles but crossing them is now a *choice*.

"Always do what you're afraid to do."

~Ralph Waldo Emerson

As a result of reading the above quote at the age of 18, I tolerated my stage fright and performed my original music on stage in front of strangers for the first time. I was eventually given my own local CATV music show and went on to play with some successful bands. I interviewed India's Prime Minister Morarji Desai at the United Nations in 1978. I tried out for the chorus but landed the lead role in a production of the musical, "Hair" in the late 70s. I recorded a few record albums and wrote some books. I was brave enough to ask my wife's telephone number the night we met back in 1979. I changed careers in my 30s. We relocated from Maine to New Mexico in 2013. All of the best things and experiences in my life have been the result of doing what I was afraid to do.

Clearly dangerous or hurtful things of which you *should* be afraid are an exception. Many people, especially those with anxiety disorders, *avoid* situations that make them anxious. The fact is,

We often get anxious about things that are important to us.

Think about it. First impressions, job interviews, performances, major purchases. The things and situations that make you nervous can be a road map to your own happiness. Don't avoid them. Learn to tolerate your anxiety. Take a risk. Your best life is always just beyond your comfort zone.

Here's one more argument: The fears you avoid become stronger. The fears you confront become weaker while *you* get stronger. It's your choice. You can expand your world or watch it shrink.

Fun with Controllers!

"Be not angry that you cannot make others as you wish them to be since you cannot make yourself as you wish to be."
~*Thomas a Kempis*

Treating anxiety became one of my specialties because I worked with it quickly and efficiently and because my light, casual personality is so counter to that of most anxiety clients, I had fun driving them nuts.

...so to speak.

The people most prone to anxiety disorders are those with an obsessive personality. We used to diagnose them with "Obsessive Personality Disorder" until the diagnosis became so common that it was reclassified as simply a "trait."

They are the "controllers," what some people call "control freaks." I'm going to spend a lot of time describing them because they comprise about 50% of my client load, and I find them fascinating. Controllers commonly believe that there is a right way to do everything, and everything else is the wrong way. They are uncomfortable looking within, for the most part, and prefer to meet their needs by changing and manipulating everything and everyone around them.

One client admitted that, when driving on a multi-lane highway, if someone drove too slowly in front of him, he'd swerve around that car, tuck in tightly, and then slow down, forcing the offending driver to slow down, "to teach them a lesson!"

He could have simply switched lanes and driven at the speed he preferred, but there was something oddly satisfying about taking charge and teaching a stranger a lesson.

That's a controller.

Controllers love to assign themselves the role of teacher or critic in relationships. Their most hurtful words come disguised as teachings, teasing or constructive criticism.

Controllers have no tolerance for blame, so they externalize it. Everything they do wrong, every misjudgment, every mistake is someone else's fault, in their mind. They are handicapped when it comes to seeing their own faults, but experts in spotting yours.

Controllers seldom apologize, and when they do, it's always followed by a detailed explanation of how what they did was completely understandable, given the circumstances.

Controller's Roommate: "Did you take the $20.00 bill I put here?"

Controller: "Yeah. I had to pay the pizza delivery guy for my pizza."

Controller's Roommate: "With *my* money?"

Controller: "I'll pay you back."

Controller's Roommate: "Why didn't you *ask*?"

Controller: "You weren't around."

Controller's Roommate: "I was in the next room!"

Controller: "The last time I asked you for money you gave me a hard time. I wasn't going to go through *that* again!"

Controller's Roommate: "You wanted $600 for a dog-grooming kit!"

Controller: "It was on sale!"

Controller's Roommate: "You don't own a dog!"

Controller: "See? This is exactly how you get!"

Controller's Roommate: "So, it's *my* fault you took my $20?"

For most controllers to say simply, "I'm sorry. I was wrong," without a detailed explanation would be pure torture. I know. I've assigned it as homework.

Controllers also have trouble relaxing, which is understandable since they spend most of their time and energy in their heads, planning, making lists, and schedules, trying to anticipate everything that might happen, trying to analyze (*anal-ize*) what you might have meant by what you said, and imagining worst-case scenarios. Controllers are sometimes chronic worriers.

I'm often asked, "*Why* do I get panic attacks?" Panic attacks are your body's way of showing you who is *really* in control.

At their core, controllers feel unsafe in this world. Since they are not comfortable looking within and changing themselves, they attempt to change others, believing that this is their way to happiness and contentment.

For example, I had a client who was a controller who had a real "thing" about people interrupting him when he was speaking. It was a real button-pusher for him. It made him nuts.

Now most of us would take steps to increase our tolerance and patience level, but not a controller. He taught his wife and kids not to interrupt him. He probably had a few friends and co-workers trained, too. The problem was, he couldn't train *everyone*. Strangers interrupted him; customers interrupted him.

What did he want from therapy?

"How can I get people to stop interrupting me?"

That's how controllers think: *"If only the rest of you would do what you should, I could be happy!"*

Of course, they can't. I've yet to meet a happy controller. They all know what the rest of us should be doing and how we should live, but they're some of the least happy people on the planet because they rely on external sources for their comfort and self-esteem, rather than carry it with them.

The positive side to controllers is that they excel in the workplace. Controllers are very responsible and take their jobs seriously. They tend to be organized, responsible, and detail-oriented.

One favorite scenario I've often used with controlling clients is the following:

You and I are janitors who clean this building each night, after hours. One night, our boss tells us, "You know how you've been instructed to leave the lights on when you leave? We're changing that. Starting tonight, at the end of your shift, we want you to go through the building and turn off all of the lights."

Now you're the controller. You take this new instruction very seriously. You may wind up spending a good amount of time pondering why management made this decision. You're guessing that it's to save on the electric bill.

I, on the other hand, am that casual, easy-going, relaxed type. When the end of our shift comes, all I'm thinking about is getting into my car and going home, which is what I do.

Now, you're feeling some resentment because that means that *you* have to go around turning off all the lights in the building. This happens all week. By now, you've built up some serious resentment (you're pissed!) because you're convinced that I *know full well* that we are supposed to be turning off those lights, and I'm leaving the task for you.

In fact, I've completely forgotten about it.

So when you finally sit me down and tell me how we should *both* be turning off the lights each night, you're even *angrier* when I reply,

"Oh, yeah! We were supposed to do that, weren't we?"

You're convinced that I knew this the whole time. You've spent hours and hours on this in your head. There is no way I didn't think about this at all! I must be pretending to have forgotten.

Actually, I *did* forget. It was of little importance to me. I reserve my cranial real estate for *essential* things, which is partly why I'm so much more relaxed than you. There is no hamster running in a little wheel up in my head. My head is used to solve actual problems when they occur. The rest of the time I do what I have to and enjoy what I can.

If it's any consolation, if they should decide to make one of us "Lead Janitor," it'll be you, not me.

And, while we're on the subject, when the company has a problem, a roomful of controllers may have a meeting and discuss it for hours without arriving at a workable solution. You'll mention it to me, and I'll have a clear solution instantly. That's the strength of *my* personality type. We're creative problem-solvers.

But I digress...

Controllers are organized and responsible and valuable in the workplace, but they often resent the rest of us for not being and thinking exactly like them.

I once treated a company manager who did nothing but complain about his employees' attitudes, priorities, and ways of doing things. I said, "Don't call yourself a manager if you only know how to manage people like yourself who don't need much managing. Managers should know how to manage *anyone* under them. When you learn to motivate people who are nothing like you, *then* you're a professional manager."

This was an exception. When I help controllers to be less controlling, I don't usually mess with their work life unless they get silly. Most controllers excel at work.

Another scenario that's fun to describe to controllers is the following: You agree to paint a windowsill and frame for $100, but the person hiring you adds that, if you can complete the job in one hour, you'll be paid $200.

Halfway into the job, a drop of white paint falls on the navy blue carpet. You wipe the spot with a rag, but that only smears it and makes the spot five times larger. You get some paint thinner and wet the rag and scrub the spot and now it has faded a bit, but it's ten times larger.

(At this point, most controllers are smiling because they recognize how they would react to this situation.)

Will you make the deadline and get the $200 or will you continue to work on getting the white stain out of that carpet?

Many clients will admit that they won't stop until that stain is completely gone. They are perfectionists. They are driven to finish what they start, even if that was a distraction. They hate interruptions because they distract so easily. Many controllers are chronically late because they convince themselves they can get 30 minute's worth of tasks done in the next ten minutes. In fact, their distractability and their tendency to obsess can make it difficult to complete ten minute's worth of tasks in ten minutes!

Now *my* personality type would paint the window, collect the $200, and say, "Oh! By the way, I spilled a drop of paint right there, but I'm sure it'll come out!"

Okay, so don't hire me as a painter.

Controllers are competitive. They need to be right, and they need to win. In the movie, "War Games," the computer comes to the conclusion that the only way to win is not to play. This is true when dealing with controllers, also. Because they're obsessive, they can and will argue until long after you're exhausted, if that's what it takes. And, unlike you, they *need* to win. The subject of the argument is less important to them than the victory. A few have admitted that they will even make up facts to win an argument, not because they believe in lying, but because making up a possible "fact" on the spot might result in a quick win. No matter how the argument turns out, controllers need to come away feeling clever and superior because this is a basic – if twisted and temporary – source of their self-esteem.

While controllers are invaluable in the workplace, they can be a pain in the ass to live with because they tend to *manage* their families as they would employees. They never come to therapy complaining that their controlling personality is the problem they need help with. They come in with anxiety disorders (panic attacks, phobias, excessive worry, obsessive thoughts, etc.) or relationship problems. In a few instances, they come in because their spouses have given them an ultimatum: Get professional help or I'm out of here! And, of course, they come in asking what they should do about their unreasonable spouses.

It's important to understand that controllers are often perfection-ists, holding themselves to impossible standards in an uncon-scious effort to please an imaginary parent in their head. They are unreasonably tough on the rest of us because they think that we should all be held to the same standards. They expect of *us* what they expect of *themselves*, however unreasonable.

Sometimes, in the course of treatment for anxiety disorders, they ask how they got this problem. That's when we have the talk about controlling personalities. Some even have the insight to ask what they can do about it.

In my early days as a clinician, I would suggest alternate ways of interacting with the people around them. "The next time your wife does X, try responding this way instead." It seldom worked, because we respond so habitually in close, established relation-ships.

Controllers tend to have what I call "shrines." Things are often arranged a specific way, furniture in a room, books in a bookcase or things on a dresser, pictures on a wall, the things on one's desk at work, etc.

What if we could increase their ability to tolerate frustration?

What if we messed with those shrines?

I developed an exercise. I would move my office telephone so that 1/3 of it hung over the edge of my desk or I would reach behind me and make the painting on the wall crooked.

"Drives you nuts, right? Let's just leave it there for the rest of the session. If you find it really bugs you, have a good laugh at yourself. Think of it as a harmless quirk of yours. You'll never wind up in a mental hospital over such a silly thing."

"When you go home today, I want you to try something. Start looking for the places where you need things to be "just so." Pick one thing that might bug you and mess it up. Put a lamp or a phone close to the edge of whatever it's sitting on. Rearrange anything in a way that makes no sense. Make a picture crooked. Change just one thing in a place where you're going to spend some time. If you find it *doesn't* bug you, choose something else. Tomorrow, you can put it back the way it was. Tomorrow, you're going to mess with *something else*. Leave dirty dishes in the sink for a day. Fail to put something away. Be sure whatever you choose *bugs you* – and just deal with it. One day only. The next day, fix it and find something else that might bother you."

People got creative with this. They would often come to their next appointment excited to tell me the creative things they did. Most were having *fun* with this!

Felix Fixate had some creative routines. His trash barrels had to touch one another when he put them in front of his house. Each piece of clothing had to touch another when he undressed for bed. The week I gave him that assignment, he had an appointment with his doctor. Being late for an appointment was unacceptable to Felix. He arrived at his doctor's office on time but didn't have any change to feed the parking meter. Normally, he would have left to get change rather than risk getting a parking ticket (also unacceptable), even if it meant being late for his appointment.

He remembered the exercise.

He reasoned that would never risk getting a parking ticket. He resigned himself to the fact that my exercise was about to cost him a $15 ticket. He left his car and kept his doctor's appointment.

He returned to his car to find he hadn't been ticketed. This led to a huge epiphany for Felix. Maybe there was only a 50/50 chance of getting a ticket. Maybe the rules of living in this world and the terrible consequences of breaking them weren't carved in stone after all.

Even I was surprised that such a minor act had led to such a huge insight. It began a reversal of all his other obsessive rituals.

The best part of my harmless little exercise was that, as people increased their frustration tolerance, they began to ease up on themselves. The more they eased up on themselves, the more they eased up on the people around them.

Controlling clients began coming to sessions reporting that their spouse or kids or coworkers or friends were noticing personality changes in them.

I just shrugged and said, "That's great." No point in telling them that it was the stupid little things like making their plastic Jesus lie down on the dashboard of their car for a day that did the trick.

Change the basic underlying personality in a way that's not terribly difficult for the client, get them to have a good laugh at themselves while doing it, and many anxiety symptoms disappear.

I'm a professional sneak.

TACKLING ANXIETY

"The task we must set for ourselves is not to feel secure, but to be able to tolerate insecurity." ~Erich Fromm

Specific Phobias

A phobia is an irrational fear that limits functioning in some way. To feel a bit nervous looking down from the roof of a skyscraper is normal. To pass up a "dream job" because your office will be on the ninth floor is not normal. To be startled to find a bumblebee on your arm is normal. To quit your job because it involves leaving your house, going to your car, and risking being stung by a bumblebee is not-quite-normal. It sounds silly when we consider that there are people who are afraid of puppies and kittens and flowers and shadows and dolls and sleep and bathing, but those fears are very real to the person experiencing them.

Hippopotomonstrosesquipedaliophobia is the fear of long words.

Specific phobias come in four flavors: Animal phobias (cats, snakes, spiders, etc.), situational phobias (driving over bridges, flying, fear of enclosed spaces, etc.), environmental phobias (heights, storms, the dark, etc.), and blood-injection-injury phobias (fears of various medical procedures).

Social phobia and *agoraphobia* are considered separately from the specific phobias because of their pervasiveness.

Children who grow up with a parent with anxiety issues are prone to them because they were raised with the clear – if unspoken – message that the world is unsafe. Phobias can also be caused by distressing incidents, like my train trestle phobia.

Phobic reactions can have physical as well as emotional symptoms. Physical symptoms might include rapid heartbeat, sweating, trembling or difficulty breathing. Emotional symptoms may include fear, panic, a strong desire to exit the situation, nausea, chest pain, lightheadedness or a feeling of helplessness, entrapment, or loss of control.

We had a mailman who had such a fear of dogs that if he saw a single dog – even a sleeping, three-legged toy poodle – anywhere on our street, he would skip delivering mail to the entire street. (Of course, he may have just been lazy and used dogs as an excuse not to deliver mail.). Let's be honest. A mailman with a fear of dogs makes as much sense as an ashtray on a motorcycle.

As in my train trestle story, exposure is the key. But we don't have to expose people to their fears in real life to combat them. We can expose them in fantasy in a safe environment to prepare them for real life exposure.

One of the many things I've learned studying Ericksonian Hypnosis is that our unconscious mind experiences and processes fantasy the same way it does reality. It's why our perception of the world and the people around us is more determined by how we think than by what we observe.

Progressive desensitization is the behavioral treatment of choice for specific phobias. In progressive desensitization, we first make a detailed list of steps leading up to the person's fear. For example, if they have a fear of flying, step one might be waking up on the morning of the flight. Another step might be sitting down to breakfast and coffee that day. Later steps would include packing, printing boarding passes, driving to the airport, the security line, hearing the boarding call, finding a seat, etc. We make as many detailed steps as possible.

Next, we need a "safe place" in fantasy. Where is my client most relaxed? On a beach? In a meadow? At Thanksgiving dinner? We have the clients close their eyes and imagine themselves in their safe place. Now we tell the clients to imagine Step 1: "You wake up the morning of your flight." We take our clients through those steps until they lift their hand or finger, indicating that they can't tolerate the anxiety any longer. Then, we tell them to return to that safe place.

The beauty of progressive desensitization is, once done in the therapy office, our clients can continue to do this during the week at home. They are usually able to go further and further through the steps. Eventually, they get on the plane. The *real* plane.

I always warn clients that they won't *love* flying. They may be uncomfortable, but they'll have the *choice* of flying. It works on any phobia. Repetition is the key.

Now and then, one has to be creative about interventions. Not everyone shows up complaining of a specific phobia of snakes or spiders or phone calls from telemarketers.

I had one client, a young man in his 20s, who froze like a statue anytime he was outdoors and it started raining (pluviophobia). It was the result of a traumatic experience he once had during a rainstorm. Years later, if he got caught in the rain, he would be paralyzed (and wet) until the rain stopped.

In his case, I created a guided fantasy. First, I got him to tell me about a girl he secretly liked in high school, one of those unrequited loves that shy guys never work up the nerve to approach. He closed his eyes, and I created a guided fantasy in which she asked him for help with some homework. They walked to his house together after school and worked on their homework assignment together. Afterward, they watched some TV, they talked, they laughed, and they finally kissed until it was time for him to walk her home.

He put his arm around her while they walked. When it began to rain, she held him tight. I described how good it felt to have her holding him so close in the rain, how good it felt to kiss her again when they reached her house, and how great he felt during the walk back home – in the rain.

It was nearly a month before it rained again, but he didn't freeze up. The rain that was so closely associated with his traumatic experience was now just rain.

Agoraphobia

People with *agoraphobia* avoid public places, crowds or any situation where they might feel trapped or fear a panic attack. They don't fear the social situation so much as being physically separated from wherever they feel safe. Untreated panic disorder often escalates into agoraphobia as the person begins avoiding the places and situations that might bring on a panic attack.

I once tried running a group therapy session for people with agoraphobia, but no one showed up.

I'm only joking. Actually, a dozen people showed up, but they all insisted on sitting nearest the door. They argued and then left.

A professor in grad school warned us never to promise the client results. I learned the opposite lesson from Milton Erickson. Clients have expectations that can often be utilized to help them achieve their goals.

When I treat clients for agoraphobia, I give them the impression that this is one of the easiest illnesses to treat, assuring them that I have a nearly 100% success rate. As a result, I have a nearly 100% success rate.

I'm not above being devious if it benefits my client.

Untreated, agoraphobia tends to be progressive. Agoraphobics will stop going to public events, restaurants, parties, stores, etc. Next, they may stop working because it means leaving the home. Once they stop leaving the home, their bedroom soon becomes their safe place. I've seen severe cases where the person spends most of the day in his or her bedroom, taking meals and even relieving themselves in their bedrooms. The world of the agoraphobic systematically becomes smaller and smaller.

People with agoraphobia see things in black and white: they are either in a safe place or an unsafe place. They don't perceive a gray area until it's thrust upon them.

Treatment involves working with that gray area.

I'll have my clients list the sort of places they cannot tolerate: restaurants, shopping malls, grocery stores, parties, etc. I help them to choose one of these (neither the most nor the least threatening) and ask them to make a trip there sometime that week.

Now, normally agoraphobic clients would get anxious at some point, then leave and return home because they can no longer tolerate the anxiety. What I ask them to do is leave *temporarily*. I instruct them to leave the building, go outside, sit on a bench or in their car, have a cigarette if they smoke, and just chill out. Relax.

When they're ready, go back inside and continue.

When they can't stand the anxiety again, they should leave temporarily and chill out again. Do this as often as needed.

The beauty of this behavioral method is that the clients are in control. It effectively increases their frustration tolerance. One key element of agoraphobia is the feeling of being trapped. Leaving the stressful situation *temporarily* teaches clients that they are *not*, in fact, trapped.

I'll often illustrate this with clients by pointing out that they are not trapped in my office. They could get up and leave anytime without even an explanation. I then point out that, even I could get up right now, leave the building, and drive home. I may not have a job tomorrow, but even I am not trapped in this situation.

I've had clients ask, "What if I'm only halfway done filling my shopping cart, and I have to leave?" I tell them to leave and walk away. No one is going to take their shopping cart. None of it has been paid for. It'll be right there when you calm down and return.

I've seen this method work with clients who hadn't left their homes for more than ten years, except to keep a rare doctor's appointment. Severe agoraphobia victims often need a friend or family member to accompany them anywhere. I've had agoraphobic clients who couldn't leave the house without an entire entourage! This method worked for those people as well.

I recall one young woman with agoraphobia (among other problems) who came to our sessions each week with her husband, mother, and aunt. The three of them would sit in our waiting room for the entire hour until her session was over. Once, the client called to cancel her appointment. Apparently her *aunt* caught a cold and couldn't come.

I once took my wife out for dinner to a Portuguese restaurant in Taunton, Massachusetts. Seated at a large nearby table was a former client who I had previously treated for agoraphobia. The man, a Portuguese immigrant, was having dinner with no less than ten family members. When he spotted me, he got up from the table and had his entire family come to meet "Dr. Rick". They each took turns shaking my hand — even the children! When I introduced my wife, people began shaking *her* hand. It was quite a funny moment, especially for my wife. When I first met this man, he hadn't dined in a restaurant in years.

Steve Stasher was easily the most severe anxiety case of my career. He wouldn't sit in our waiting room if there were one other person in the room. In torrential downpours, he would wait outside until I came to get him.

When he and his younger sister were six and four years old, their single mother would leave them alone in a motel room for as much as two weeks at a time with only a bag or two of groceries. At the age of 26, my client needed to hide food under a mattress, tucked into seat cushions, etc., anywhere that he slept. He felt a sense of security knowing that food was nearby.

Steve described how he and his sister often ran out of toilet paper in whatever motel room they found themselves. Their mother arranged that no housekeeping service would enter and clean the room. The children were under strict orders never to leave the motel room or talk with anyone. Steve was fitted with orthodontic braces, at one point. His mother never brought him for any follow-up appointments and, over the years, his teeth rotted underneath the braces.

To treat his agoraphobia, I told him to go to the local mall and walk around until he couldn't stand it anymore, then go outside, sit on a bench, relax, then go back inside when ready. Repeat as necessary.

When I saw him the following week, his entire demeanor had changed. He was more relaxed but walked and talked more energetically. I asked how his visit to the mall had been.

"It was great! It sucked at first. I had to leave every five minutes or so, and then it would take me at least 20 minutes before I could go back in. Eventually, I was able to stay a lot longer."

"How long did you do this for?"

"I spent the whole afternoon last Sunday. Four hours."

Now I would *never* ask a client to do this for four hours. I consider tolerating this exercise for less than an hour a victory because I know it's going to work. But I didn't suggest a time frame, and he chose to spend the afternoon at it. Who cares? It worked!

A month later he sat with thousands of spectators at a major NASCAR event. He had been a race car fan for years but could never tolerate even a small local race in person. A year later, at the age of 27, he applied for and landed his first job ever – working at the pet store of that same mall.

Social Phobia

"The deepest fear we have, 'the fear beneath all fears,' is the fear of not measuring up, the fear of judgment." ~*Tullian Tchividjian*

People with *social phobia* have a crippling fear of being judged or embarrassed in common social situations. Will I sound intelligent? Will I act withdrawn? Will people know how nervous I am? They might worry for days (or weeks) because they have to attend a party where they'll have to eat and drink in front of other people. Even explaining that they ate before the party might be humiliating to someone with social phobia. They are perceived by most as simply shy, but most of them are secretly horrified when you single them out and introduce yourself. They do everything they can to avoid social situations.

The three most effective treatments for social phobia are cognitive therapy, exposure therapy, and social anxiety groups. *Cognitive therapy* does a great job of helping clients see the unconscious beliefs that fuel their fears.

Q. "What is the worst that could happen if you attended the conference next week?"

A. "I'd act really awkward and withdrawn."

Q. "And what is the worst that could happen if you acted awkwardly and withdrawn?"

A. "I'd feel embarrassed and humiliated."

Q. "And what is the worst that could happen if you felt embarrassed and humiliated?"

A. "Everyone would hate me! They would think I was ridiculous. They would all be laughing at me."

Q. "So, a roomful of strangers would hate you and laugh at you if you acted shy and awkward. You expect that you would make that big an impact? Okay. Let's assume that's true. Everyone in the room hates you and is laughing at you because you seem shy. Is there anything you can do to prevent that from happening?"

I'm over-simplifying, but this is how these dialogues often go.

Exposure therapy helps the most compliant and motivated social anxiety sufferers. We make a list of fearful social situations and rank them in order of the anxiety they produce. Then we ask the client to tolerate the mildest ones on the list. As the client succeeds, we work our way up the list. The problem inherent in exposure therapy is the client's reluctance to interact with strangers.

Social Anxiety group therapy can be particularly effective because each client gets to interact socially in what becomes a safe and controlled setting with others who suffer from the same illness.

Panic Disorder

As mentioned earlier, anxiety is a normal human emotion. It increases our adrenaline production to improve our chances in a fight or flight situation. But, while I take steps to calm myself during an anxiety-producing situation, people with anxiety disorders do the opposite. They make themselves more anxious. They worry more, obsess more, flee the situation, or, in the case of panic disorder, instead of calming themselves, they convince themselves that something is terribly wrong. They tell themselves they must be having a heart attack or a "nervous breakdown" which is as effective as using gasoline to put out a fire.

A panic or anxiety attack is an emotional false alarm. The sufferers convince themselves that they're in a fight or flight situation when there is no threat, no danger. Nothing is happening except in the person's mind. The person feels a bit of normal anxiety, or notices a rapid heartbeat, or sweaty palms, or some rapid breathing, or obsessive thinking, or worry, and begins to fear a panic attack coming on, which, of course, triggers the panic attack.

My goal in treating panic attacks is to teach the client to turn them off. However, different things work for different people. I have to find what will work for each person. Once a client has turned off a few panic attacks successfully, there is no reason for them to occur anymore. They just stop happening.

My basic approach to treating panic disorder is threefold. In Week One I teach clients diaphragmatic breathing (breathing from the stomach instead of the chest) and instruct them to practice it regularly while watching TV, reading, in a waiting room, etc. The goal is to become so comfortable doing it that you can easily do it at the first sign of a panic attack. When a panic attack occurs, the client who has practiced begins the diaphragmatic breathing. This does two things: it counters the typically shallow breathing that often accompanies a panic attack and puts the client back in control. This is a behavioral approach.

I had one client who responded to this so well that she came to her next appointment and said, "For 25 years I've seen psychiatrists, psychologists, social workers, all kinds of professionals. I've taken every possible medication. I've talked about my childhood until I was sick of hearing my own voice! Why didn't any of *them* teach me this stupid breathing trick?"

Who knew that the first thing we tried would work?

Some people have trouble with behavioral interventions. They either tell themselves that the suggestion won't work, or they don't bother trying the breathing until they're in the midst of a panic attack (when they're too panicked to do it). Some clients are so up in their heads that they have lost the ability to modify their behavior in any meaningful way.

For this reason, in Week Two, I switch to a cognitive intervention: distraction. Based on the client's interests, I might instruct the client to make a mental list at the first sign of a panic attack. List all the James Bond movies you can think of. Name every Beatles song you can. List every breakfast cereal, or every local street name, whatever. The point is to make a list that you have to think about. This derails the panic attack by replacing the fearful obsession with a harmless one. Of course, some clients don't bother to try this, either, and some just lack the ability to take any control of themselves during a panic attack. For them, there's Week Three: Transcendental Meditation.

Transcendental Meditation has been around for many years. It was introduced in the US by Maharishi Mahesh Yogi of India back in the 1950's. I learned it in 1971 at a cost of $35. I was also required to bring an offering of flowers to be placed in front of the Maharishi's picture. That part of it was very silly, but the meditation method was quite powerful.

At the time, the TM people were making all sorts of extraordinary claims about TM. Experienced meditators needed less sleep and could control autonomic functions such as their pulse and blood pressure. Harvard Professor, Dr. Herbert Benson, set out to disprove the TM claims by studying experienced meditators with brain and body monitoring equipment. After extensive testing, when many of those claims turned out to be true, Dr. Benson added a minor element to it and wrote his own book, calling it "The Relaxation Response."

When I was in grad school and our professor said we were going to discuss and learn "The Relaxation Response," I was the troublemaker who raised his hand and asked, "Don't you mean Transcendental Meditation?"

I won't go into all of the reported benefits of TM. You can find that online. When practiced 15 to 20 minutes daily for several months, TM can decrease a person's general anxiety level. Not everyone is willing to interrupt his day to meditate for 15 to 20 minutes, but those who do get relief from panic attacks and all sorts of anxiety issues.

One of the reasons that TM is most effective for people with anxiety disorders is that there is no internal counting involved, as in many other meditation methods. When anxious or obsessive people lose track of their count, which is normal, they tend to get anxious about it, breaking them out of their meditation.

I've taught TM to many clients in 30 minutes. Today, the Maharishi Foundation USA charges anywhere from $950 - $1500 to teach it to you. At those prices, I hope you don't still have to bring flowers.

Clients who still have panic attacks for whatever reason after six weeks or so are given an appointment to see a psychiatrist. Most psychiatrists will prescribe benzodiazepine (anti-anxiety) drugs (e.g. alprazolam, clonazepam, lorazepam, diazepam, etc.) I consider this a last resort because these drugs are so addictive with regular use. Also, the anxiety clients who manage to be successfully weaned off of these drugs frequently experience worse anxiety symptoms and disorders than they had in the first place. I often ask psychiatrists I work with to first prescribe non-addictive paroxetine (Paxil), an anti-depressant with an anti-anxiety side-effect.

During my first year of practice, I got a client with a history of panic attacks. No problem. I was getting pretty good at teaching people tricks to turn off their panic attacks. But none worked on this woman. She refused to consider medication. I read everything I could find about treating panic attacks to see if I had missed something.

Then, one afternoon, she talked about how she "*helped Mommy*" with chores around her house. "*Helped Mommy*" seemed so out of character for this 40-something-year-old, well-educated woman. I began asking pointed questions about her childhood.

She avoided mentioning it in the past, but it turned out her abusive mother would routinely force her to hold her pee for absurd lengths of time. Failure to hold it resulted in a beating. Once, when my client was eight-years-old and suffering from the flu, the family flew her to Florida and left her alone in their hotel room every day while the rest of them vacationed at the beach. She was so sick by the time they returned home; she had to be hospitalized.

I learned that there were panic attacks, and there were panic attacks. The common type was relatively easy to treat. The kind that stemmed from severe trauma was not. With these, you have to deal with the trauma first. Only then, do the panic attacks go away.

Exception noted. Lesson learned.

Obsessive-Compulsive Disorder

Obsessive-Compulsive Disorder (OCD) is a condition in which the sufferers not only have anxiety-producing obsessions but are *forced to carry out specific repetitive behaviors to alleviate their anxiety.*

Examples include:

➤ Germaphobes who feel the compulsion to wash their hands every time they touch anything.

➤ People who, while trying to get to sleep, begin to wonder if they turned off the oven or locked the front door. They may have checked this four times already but – what if they only *dreamed* they checked it? They get out of bed and check it again.

➤ The person who has to do everything an even (or odd) number of times.

➤ The person who feels compelled to arrange physical objects in a (perceived) orderly or symmetrical fashion.

➤ The person who fears losing control (e.g., harming oneself or others, stealing, shouting, etc.)

➤ Irrational counting: ceiling tiles, white automobiles, bricks in a wall, steps while walking, etc.

➤ Disturbing thoughts. These often take the form of aggressive, sexual, or religious thoughts and can be associated with all sorts of compulsive behaviors.

People with OCD can be very original and creative about their obsessions and compulsions, making it difficult to categorize all of the possibilities.

In Maine, I shared my office with a female therapist, Lena Lemonface, who I only met once because we worked on different days. On the desk, she kept a big bottle of that waterless hand cleaner that's so popular. She would occasionally leave me a note to tell me to feel free to use it anytime. I thought that was nice of her, but I don't like using that stuff because it's alcohol-based and alcohol dries out the skin, and I'm too much of a "guy" to use hand lotion to counteract the damage.

There was tape on the arms of our office chair. I assumed it was a poor attempt to repair damaged leather. I found it annoying because the tape was loose and made a distracting noise when I moved my arms. One day, I decided to re-tape the arms of the chair. I got some good, strong nylon tape and proceeded to remove the old tape.

Surprise! There was nothing wrong with the arms of the chair. Lena had OCD! She was a germaphobe. The tape was there to protect her from *Rick cooties*! It was loose because she removed it every time *she* used the office. Then, of course, it occurred to me that the occasional notes were not because she was generous with her precious waterless hand cleaner. It was to keep my cooties off our telephone, and desk, and anything else in the shared office that I might touch.

Months later, she resigned. When I asked our support staff the reason, I was told that someone had borrowed our office chair a month ago. Lena had complained that the borrower had adjusted the chair, and she couldn't get it back the way it was. Lena insisted the agency buy her a new chair. The agency invited her to switch it with any other chair in the agency. Lena quit.

I felt better knowing that it wasn't only *my* cooties that repulsed her.

I'll admit I did notice a slight difference in the chair's adjustment. It was worth a whole five seconds of my attention.

But I digress...

Like most phobias and panic attacks, OCD is often an overreaction to a non-threatening event. Let's be realistic: if I forget to lock the front door when I go to bed tonight, in all likelihood a burglar or a serial killer won't pick tonight to pay me a visit.

That isn't the OCD sufferer's logic. OCD sufferers react as though a break-in is a foregone conclusion. Unless they carry out the compulsive behavior (checking the door for the fifth time), either the worst will happen, or they will be unable to get to sleep due to the anxious, obsessive thoughts.

In many cases, people with OCD are cognitively aware that their compulsive behaviors are silly and useless, but *they do them because it is the only way they know to alleviate the anxiety produced by their obsession.*

The therapeutic approach of choice is called exposure and response prevention therapy. We begin by making a list of the client's compulsive behaviors. Then we rank these behaviors by the relative amount of anxiety associated with them.

We choose a compulsive behavior that is associated with a relatively low amount of anxiety and identify the obsessive *triggers* that lead to that behavior. Then we get the client to agree *not* to respond to that trigger with the compulsive behavior for as long as possible.

For example, Billy Butterfinger picks his nose whenever he sees a pretty woman. We have determined that, of all his compulsive behaviors, this one is fairly mild. (Of course, pretty women may disagree on this point). On Billy's relative anxiety scale from 1 to 10, this ranks only a two. We get him to agree to refrain from picking his nose the next time he sees a pretty woman. In some cases, depending on the compulsive behavior, we can begin this during the client's treatment session. In all cases, we are going to ask the client to do this on his own between sessions.

This is difficult at first. The brain is hard-wired to expect that only the compulsive behavior will alleviate the anxiety caused by the trigger. As the client practices this, the brain begins to get the message that nothing catastrophic happens when the compulsive behavior does not occur. Eventually, the compulsion becomes one of many simple options. When we have successfully combated a compulsion brought on by a mild amount of anxiety, most clients are now very motivated to tackle their more moderate to severe compulsions.

However, some people have real trouble adjusting their behavior. They tell themselves it won't work, or that they won't survive the anxiety. In these cases, as well as severe cases where the compulsive behaviors threaten the person's health, there is:

Medication

Medication is a touchy subject. On one hand, there are doctors who would be happy to medicate you for life, so you never have to suffer a sad or boring day. On the other hand, there are those who believe that all medication is a conspiracy of the big pharmaceutical firms to make a buck and enslave the masses.

Like most people, I'm somewhere in between.

Medication is necessary. I wouldn't medicate *every* case of mental illness, only the severe ones, and ones that are resistant to therapy. I don't want to see my anxiety clients medicated until all means of psychotherapy fails.

Schizophrenics need anti-psychotics. Mood-disordered clients need mood stabilizers. I've seen very few exceptions.

However, I'm skeptical about medicating six-year-old boys for ADHD while continuing to feed them cola, coffee, and energy drinks. When I was a child, all mothers knew that caffeine over-stimulated the developing hearts of young children. Today, "energy drinks" have become a 50 billion dollar industry with most of their marketing aimed at young people.

I was skeptical decades ago when stressed housewives were given long-term prescriptions for diazepam (Valium) to help them get numbly through the day.

Have you ever read the fine print in those information sheets that accompany prescription drugs? I don't mean the Cliff Notes version you get from your pharmacy but the sheet with the microscopic print that comes from the manufacturer. Hidden in all that scientific language is a statement such as, "...in clinical trials, 35% of subjects responded favorably to placebos while 41% of subjects given this drug responded favorably, thus proving the efficacy of the drug."

In other words, 35% of test subjects got relief from the pain or depression from taking a sugar pill. The very idea that relief was on the way was enough to cause their brain to release the proper chemicals that supplied the relief. But this medication, which tries to artificially stimulate the release of those same brain chemicals, does a tiny bit better, justifying its $200 a month cost.

There are scientists out there who have been diligently studying the placebo effect for decades but, not surprisingly, considerably more money is invested in pharmaceutical research and development.

On the other hand — here come the pitchforks and torches — I'm also skeptical about herbal remedies and supplements. There remains no hard evidence that most of these have any effectiveness treating anything. What they *do* have going for them is the benefit of the placebo effect.

Announce that wearing a pyramid hat or eating tulip petals or rubbing a chicken bone on your knee promotes wellness and a feeling of well-being and watch how many people try it and swear that it changed their lives.

Herbal cures and supplements have become a 34 billion dollar industry in the US, propelled by the public's distrust of the pharmaceutical industry and the willingness to believe in unconfirmed junk science. Only about one-third of these supplements have ever been tested for safety and efficacy. According to Representative Henry Waxman, D-Calif., who advocates for stricter regulation of supplements, "The alternative medicine industry is as tough as any industry I've seen lobby in Washington. They have a lot of money at stake. They want to maximize their profits, and they want as little regulation as possible."

I had a schizoaffective client in his 20s whose parents took him off his mood stabilizer in favor of monthly colonics and St. John's Wort. The result was devastating. He walked up to a woman's car at a stop light, at a busy intersection, opened her driver's side door, and attempted to molest her in broad daylight.

The most common assumption in the argument against pharmaceutical medication is:

Pharmaceuticals = synthetic = bad.
Herbal = natural = good.

Cytosar-U, a staple pharmaceutical for treating leukemia and lymphoma is a chemical found in a Caribbean sea sponge while the insulin that so many Type I diabetics rely on has been synthetic for decades. Hemlock, Wolfsbane, Horse Chestnuts, Wild Carrot, Meadow Saffron, and Belladonna are all natural – and all deadly poisons. "All Natural" has become a marketing hook.

Some pharmaceuticals are plant-based while the production and testing of alternative herbal remedies remain unregulated. The issue is just not as simple as people would like to believe.

Another marketing hook is the claim that we should all be eating the same diet our ancestors ate. Despite the claims of the "Paleo Diet" promoters, paleoanthropologists have rarely seen the remains of a caveman who lived to age 40. In the mid-1500s, the world average life expectancy was 55 years, if we don't count the children who died before the age of five. Today, that world average life expectancy is 83*.

*The average life expectancy in the US is only 79. People in Japan, Australia, Canada and most of Europe (the countries with Universal Health Care) outlive us by as much as five years.

But I digress once again...

In the case of severe OCD, pharmaceutical drugs like fluvox-amine, fluoxetine, paroxetine, sertraline, and clomipramine are commonly prescribed.

I knew a young guy with an unusual complaint. He had two small clocks in his living room. They were the type with little plastic flaps that dropped down showing the minutes and hours. Each minute, when the flap on one clock would drop, he would wait for the other clock's flap to drop. He could be in mid-conversation or watching TV. No matter what he was doing his compulsion was to stop every minute when he heard that "click" and wait for the other "click."

His psychiatrist prescribed fluvoxamine (Luvox). After some weeks, the drug kicked in, and the guy was a bit less bothered by the sound of those clocks.

Like many drugs of this type, the *possible* side effects of this one may include:

> ➢ Extreme worry
>
> ➢ Depression
>
> ➢ Thoughts of harming yourself
>
> ➢ Panic attacks
>
> ➢ Agitation or irritability
>
> ➢ Difficulty falling asleep or staying asleep
>
> ➢ Aggressive behaviors

➢ Severe restlessness

➢ Acting without thinking

➢ Frenzied, abnormal excitement

Funny that no one thought to suggest he simply remove one of the clocks from his living room.

Pharmaceuticals are vital. But they are not the answer to every mental health complaint. Neither are herbal remedies.

Generalized Anxiety Disorder

Meet the chronic worriers. They spend most of their lives in the prison of their own thoughts. They live in a state of constant apprehension or dread. They have no tolerance for uncertainty. They may feel it's their fault when anything bad happens. They may be perfectionists. They probably grew up with the message that the world is unsafe and now waste their lives anticipating every catastrophic possibility imaginable. This requires some serious mental real estate which would be better served interacting with real life in the real world.

While most of us might worry and go into a problem-solving mode when an actual problem arises, chronic worriers obsessively think up new things to worry about. They imagine problems that don't exist and then spend time trying to solve them and fretting over the worse-case scenarios.

Chronic worriers wind up disconnected from real life. They filter all experience through their thought processes. People with Generalized Anxiety Disorder feel safer experiencing life from a distance through the fantasy world of the mind than they do being in the present moment. The act of overthinking is an unconscious way of *avoiding feelings*. Emotions about avoided issues are transformed into useless thoughts such as guilt and needless worry which are unresolvable because they mask deeper issues.

People with GAD often have trouble sleeping, relaxing, or concentrating. Physical symptoms can include headaches, muscle tension, fatigue, nausea, and agitation. Because GAD sufferers spend most of their time in their heads, it's no surprise that cognitive therapy tends to be the best treatment of choice.

The only behavioral component I use in the treatment of GAD is to teach some relaxation exercises since worriers have difficulty relaxing. Teaching relaxation is not as easy as it would seem. There are lots of relaxation techniques out there but, like therapy itself, what works for one client may not work for another. It is *our* job as therapists to know enough options to find which works. I have brought my own personal biofeedback devices into the office for several clients who needed to see tangible evidence of their agitated state vs. their relaxed state.

After helping the chronic worrier find and learn a relaxation exercise or two, it's time for the cognitive components of the treatment. I'll often ask the client to make a written list of all the worries that come into his mind, now in the office and then add to that list throughout her week. Then, in the next session, we discuss whether each item is an immediate and solvable problem as well as the likelihood of each worst-case scenario. We do this weekly to teach clients to look at their thoughts this way. It also helps clients become more comfortable letting go of things over which they have no control.

Another intervention that works for some GAD sufferers is designating a "worry period". Clients are instructed to make a note reminding them of an issue when they catch themselves worrying or solving non-existent problems and delay all worrying until a specific hour of the day. I suggest designating a 30-minute period in the evening. When the 30 minutes is over, all worries get shelved until the next evening.

Because chronic worriers always focus on possible future problems, they tend to be out of touch with the present. It helps to focus on questions like, "What can you do to improve your life/happiness/contentment/relationships/marriage/satisfaction *right now*?" For this same reason, any mindfulness training helps.

If I can get the client to combine mindfulness with physical exercise, so much the better. Focusing one's attention on the soles of one's feet while walking or on one's breathing while doing any exercise is extremely beneficial for all anxiety and depressive disorders.

We need to get people out of their heads and into the present moment in the real world.

Also, I try getting clients with anxiety issues to limit their caffeine and sugar intake, caffeine because it increases *all* anxiety symptoms and sugar because it causes blood-sugar levels to spike and crash, adding to fatigue.

Oh...Loosen UP!

"A sense of humor is the best indicator that you will recover; it is often the best indicator that people will love you. Sustain that and you have hope." ~Andrew Solomon

One of my favorite aspects of working with anxiety disorders is getting all those controllers to loosen up. Yes, the artwork in my office was set up to drive them nuts, and I would often give them exercises that would mess with their sense of organization. But sometimes they needed more.

Remember, these were people who took themselves and life itself very seriously. Some of them needed some real shaking up, so they got some really nutty tasks for homework:

1) When you do your dishes (or laundry, or dusting, etc.), do it as a ballet.

2) Drive to work wearing a silly hat and a fake mustache. Be sure the mustache *looks* fake.

3) Call and order a pizza but, when asked for your name, give them a ridiculously silly name like, "Twitwiggle." Then go and pick up your pizza and proudly announce your name as "Twitwiggle."

4) Sing out loud in public when people least expect it. Give yourself extra points if the song is ridiculous.

5) Make a list of the funniest things that ever happened to you.

6) Smile and say hello to at least four strangers in one day.

7) Call random phone numbers and politely ask whoever answers what time it is. (This only worked pre-Caller ID.)

8) Post-Caller ID version: Approach four strangers and ask what time it is.

9) Over the next week, do four things you have never done before.

10) The next time you get a call from a telemarketer, no matter what he or she says, order a pepperoni pizza with extra cheese.

11) At any random grocery store bring a box of Cheerios to any store employee and ask (very seriously) "Excuse me. Are these donut seeds?"

12) When you arrive for next week's appointment, hand everyone in the waiting room a candy. On the following week, hand everyone a balloon.

13) Superglue a quarter to the floor in a mall or on a sidewalk. Stand on it while the glue sets. Then sit nearby and watch people try to get it.

14) At McDonald's, order a Whopper, or at Burger King, order a Big Mac. Play innocent: "You don't sell Big Macs anymore??"

15) The next time you're driving in your car, wave to four random people as if you know them.

16) The next time you're in a store's dressing room yell, "Hey! There's no toilet paper in here!"

There were much more of these. In all fairness, I would usually suggest three to five of these and let my client choose which one to do. The ridiculous ones make the others seem reasonable in comparison. (Although I recall several clients who had so much fun doing the one they chose they did more of them that week.) The point was to get people to play, to do something they would never do. The power of the exercise was to realize that they survived the silly behavior. The world did not fall apart because they had stepped out of character.

NO FUN TREATING PTSD

There are stressors, and there are stressors, from the life-threatening to the merely inconvenient. And each of us has a varying degree of coping skills to deal emotionally with our stressors. When a particular life-threatening (or even *perceived* life-threatening) inescapable traumatic event is more than we can handle emotionally, imagine a thick glass wall drops down between our conscious self and our emotions. It allows us to survive the threat. If I can no longer *feel* what's happening, I can better survive it.

The problem is, when the threat has passed, that thick, glass wall remains stuck in place. We can no longer access our normal emotions, except anger and fear. Our fear and anger, and in some cases, sadness, now always seem to be lurking beneath the surface.

Emotions like joy and happiness remain on the other side of that wall. The people in our lives are on the other side of that wall. That's PTSD. Most PTSD symptoms make perfect sense if you imagine the victim trapped behind that glass wall. It's the result of experiencing extreme trauma with which they were not emotionally equipped to cope.

The PTSD victims I'm most experienced treating are rape victims, incest survivors, and combat veterans. They usually come to therapy complaining about their temper, trust issues, relationship difficulties, intrusive thoughts, etc.

To diagnose PTSD, certain conditions must be met.

The client may have: (one required)

> Directly experienced the traumatic event;

> Witnessed the traumatic event in person;

> Learned that the violent or accidental traumatic event occurred to a close family member or close friend

> Experienced first-hand repeated or extreme exposure to aversive details of the traumatic event

The disturbance must cause significant distress or impairment in the individual's social interactions, the capacity to work, or other important areas of functioning. Actual symptoms fall into four categories:

Re-experiencing symptoms: (one required)

> Recurrent, involuntary, and intrusive memories.

> Traumatic nightmares

> Dissociative reactions (e.g., flashbacks)

> Something that you see, hear, or smell can cause you to relive the event. This is called a **trigger.**

> Physiological response after exposure to trauma-related stimuli.

Avoidance symptoms: (one required)

> Persistent trauma-related thoughts or feelings;

➤ Persistent trauma-related external reminders (e.g., people, places, conversations, activities, objects, or situations).

Negative symptoms: (two required)

➤ Inability to recall key features of the traumatic event (not due to head injury, alcohol, or drugs).

➤ Persistent (and often distorted) negative beliefs and expectations about oneself or the world.

➤ Persistent blame of self or others for causing the traumatic event or for the resulting consequences.

➤ Persistent negative trauma-related emotions (e.g., fear, horror, anger, guilt, or shame).

➤ Markedly diminished interest in previously enjoyable activities.

➤ Feeling alienated from others.

➤ persistent inability to experience positive emotions.

Hyperarousal symptoms: (two required)

➤ Irritable or aggressive behavior.

➤ Self-destructive or reckless behavior.

➤ **Hypervigilance. The need to see what is going on around you at all times.**

➤ **Exaggerated startle response.**

➤ **Problems concentrating**

➤ **Problems sleeping.**

At the risk of getting boring and technical, each symptom must have lasted for at least a month, and the person must experience symptoms from each of the four categories. Also, the trauma itself must have occurred more than three months ago. (If it happened less than three months ago it is "Acute Stress Disorder.") I mention these factors because I've known licensed professionals who get this wrong.

To complicate matters further, psychiatrist and author Judith Herman developed the term "Complex PTSD", or C-PTSD to describe traumatic conditions that do not fully meet the above criteria or have symptoms atypical of PTSD. This diagnosis name has not been officially accepted because it describes what is traditionally diagnosed as, "Disorder of Extreme Stress, not otherwise specified." Nonetheless, there are clients, as well as clinicians, who use the term. I suspect that had Judith called it "PTSD Lite," the name would have been considerably less popular.

You can almost spot PTSD sufferers. In public places like waiting rooms, they never close their eyes and relax. They always choose a seat with their backs to a wall so that they can see a maximum number of people and see whoever enters the room. They are very protective of their personal space, and they startle easily. If you come up behind them quietly and put your hand on their shoulder, be prepared to peel them off the ceiling. They often have little patience for "small talk" and tend to keep their physical and emotional distance.

I once did an intake on a young man who came to the Vet Center hoping to be eligible for veteran's benefits. He claimed to suffer from PTSD as a result of his Army service during Operation

Desert Storm and said he lost the paperwork that would prove his service. I suspected that he was lying long before he described beheading the enemy and hanging their heads from the doors of their thatched huts. This young man had watched way too many Vietnam movies. Thatched huts in the desert? For those who don't recall, Desert Storm was essentially a 100 hour-long, highly technological 'war' in which we killed more U.S. troops than the enemy did.

What tipped me off that he was lying was the simple fact that he pulled his chair up close to mine at the start of the interview. People with PTSD need lots of personal space and will not casually invade the personal space of a stranger.

Traditionally, clinicians used to treat trauma clients by having them describe the trauma week after week. Many still do. One rationale was that it would desensitize the client. Another rationale was that the client would be able to release all those pent-up feelings in the safety of the office and move on. As a result, the client was re-injured week after week. The client would leave the office emotionally shattered, with many vital defenses broken down, and with no symptom relief in sight.

I always avoid re-injuring trauma victims. Since trust is an issue for most PTSD clients, I focus first on establishing a relationship. I'll ask what category the trauma falls into (sexual trauma, violent trauma, war-related trauma, etc.), but I don't press for details, even when my employer insists that I do. I make it clear to clients that at any time if they wish to discuss details, I'll listen. As we meet on a weekly schedule, my goal is to win the client's trust. I want the client to be very comfortable with me. We discuss relationships, work, play, whatever the client wishes to discuss.

I might teach some practical relaxation and anger management skills. The client may bring up some guilt or shame issues, common with PTSD. As I do with paranoid schizophrenics, I look for one small thing that I can help with, something easy for the client to fix. This is often the biggest step toward gaining my client's trust. "If this therapist knew how to fix my problem with my co-worker, maybe he knows his stuff.

"Maybe he's smarter than he looks."

And maybe now I have a client who trusts me enough to work on the *big* issue.

Aside from the old Freudian strategy of "Let's-Talk-It-To-Death-And-Hope-It-Goes-Away", today we have techniques collectively known as "power therapies" for treating trauma. I expect that lots of clinicians will disagree with me, but we have my hero, Milton Erickson, to thank for each one of the power therapies. Dr. Erickson was the most talented psychotherapist of all time.

Milton Erickson was dyslexic and color blind and developed polio at the age of 17. Back when psychiatrists were still talking with people for a 50-minute hour, Erickson was reinventing therapy. He was the originator of *"Brief Therapy"* and *"Solution-Focused Therapy"*. On countless occasions, he would see a client in one single visit and plant a single thought or give them a single assignment that would accomplish exactly what they needed. Some excellent books were written documenting these creative and brilliant sessions of his. Check out *Uncommon Therapy* by Jay Haley to read some of Erickson's cases and surprising interventions.

Throughout my career, whenever I was asked my "professional development goal" at employee review time, I grinned and replied, "I want to be Milton Erickson. I want to be able to help people in one single session." My clinical supervisors always laughed, but they knew I meant it.

As I learned in grad school, "There are 37 ways to entrance someone in hypnotherapy, and Milton Erickson is responsible for 36 of them." One of Erickson's 36 methods was distraction. Today, we have to ask a client's permission to use hypnotherapy. There were no such laws in Erickson's day. Dr. Erickson might ask clients to look at a clock or a spot on the wall while he talked. Then he would use the cadence of his speech to put them into a trance. He spoke directly to his client's unconscious mind while all defenses were down. Erickson would plant the seed that, once grown, would repair the dysfunction.

He was that good.

The most famous and popular of the power therapies is Eye Movement Desensitization and Reprocessing (EMDR) therapy. In EMDR, the therapy session takes place while the clients focus their attention on the therapist's finger which is moving left to right to left in front of their eyes.

Sounds kinda distracting, huh?

EMDR has been intricately developed into eight phases of treatment, which, I suppose, keeps it from looking too much like Ericksonian Hypnotherapy. Don't get me wrong. I'm not suggesting that EMDR doesn't work. Of *course,* it works! I'm just suggesting that anytime you practice psychotherapy while distracting the client, you have Dr. Erickson to thank.

Another power therapy is "Thought Field Therapy" (TFT) or "Emotional Freedom Technique" (EFT). TFT was the brainchild of Roger Callahan, who first introduced it as a diet method and then expanded it once he realized it was effective for anxiety, PTSD, and all sorts of other applications. EFT and other tapping techniques were later introduced by some of Roger's blessed disciples.

In all of these tapping therapies, the client taps his finger on various parts of his face and body while repeating positive and appropriate therapeutic affirmations.

This sounds distracting, too, huh?

TFT and EFT are not simple. Heavens, no. The particular spots that you tap are "meridian points" based on the same ancient Chinese energy system chart used in acupuncture. What you are doing is fixing your own emotional and mental state by rerouting your energy flow without needles.

At least, that's the hype.

Dr. Callahan took this one step further. He decided there were "algorithms." One poked in this order for this ailment and that order for that ailment. The founder of EFT disagreed and tossed out the algorithms. I prefer simplicity, myself.

Do TFT and EFT work? Absolutely. But, no matter how much lipstick you put on that pig, it's still pork.

Milton Erickson was a genius. If you plan to profit from discoveries he gave the world for free, you must first dress them up, so no one recognizes them.

In the 1970s, Richard Bandler and John Grinder studied the work of Virginia Satir, Fritz Perls, and Milton Erickson, who they considered the leaders in psychotherapy. From their studies and interviews, they developed Neuro-Linguistic Programming (NLP). NLP included a series of original psychotherapy techniques based on principles they had learned from the three practitioners.

The NLP movement produced many wonderfully effective techniques. But, toward the late '70s, Bandler and Grinder started changing NLP's focus to benefit business and sales people. A lucrative move but NLP received criticism for adding new elements for which there was no verifiable evidence. "How to Sell and Become Wealthy Using NLP!" doesn't instill much professional credibility. New people later jumped onto the NLP bandwagon developing their own sets of techniques, "How to Seduce a Girl Using NLP!" is my favorite example. By the mid-'80s, NLP lost much respect and hope as a serious source of psychotherapeutic techniques.

...but not before I stumbled onto the Visual Kinesthetic Dissociation (VKD) technique.

At the time, I was working with rape and incest victims at my mental health agency and with combat veterans at the Vet Center. TFT was proving effective with agency clients, but hardened combat vets felt it was silly. The VA was beginning to support EMDR by sending us for training, but insurance companies and Medicare weren't willing to pay for EMDR treatment yet, so it couldn't be practiced in the agency.

Enter VKD. Call it "guided visualization", and you pretty much sum it up. You don't even have to hide the fact that it was based on one of Milton Erickson's other hypnotherapy techniques. Modern NLP practitioners have tried refining it. In England, it is known as the "Rewind Technique." I found a way of practicing the original technique that sexual trauma victims and combat veterans were comfortable with. I came up with a "Lite" version I used for minor problems. It let me teach clients a handy self-directed skill and test VKD's potential effectiveness on severe PTSD clients.

"VKD Lite"

Think of something that happened to you over the past month that's still bugging you, especially if it's something that still makes you feel angry or frustrated when you think about it now.

Assign it a relative value from 0 to 10. Zero meaning that you feel no emotion at all and 10 being the most upset you have ever felt in your life. This is called the *Subjective Units of Distress Scale* (SUDS).

Turn the original incident into a very short movie in your mind, no more than a minute long. Where did this take place? Who was there? What was the conversation or incident? Remember, you're not doing this with major trauma, just a relatively recent memory that still bugs you.

Now, you're going to close your eyes and play that little "movie" quickly in your mind, but you're going to add a musical score. I want you to think of the silliest and most ridiculous piece of music you can. If the music makes you chuckle, even better.

After you have closed your eyes and played the little movie with the silly music in the background, on a scale of 0 to 10, how upset does the memory make you *now*?

Let's say it went from a four to a two. We'll run the little movie again, but this time, we're going to turn the person in the movie into the silliest cartoon character you can think of, an established cartoon character or one of your own design, it doesn't matter as long as it's ridiculous. Close your eyes, and run the new version of your movie with the cartoon character *and* the goofy music. While clients carry out this exercise, if I see a faint smile or a chuckle, I know that all is well. When they finish, I ask for a number from 0 to 10 again.

We can be creative with this by turning the entire scene into a drawing, putting a funny hat on an antagonist, or making him naked. The possibilities are endless. All of these things are dissociating clients from their negative emotions. I tell them that the memory was filed under Hurtful or Upsetting and now we've simply re-filed it. We've taken the sting out of the memory. The beauty of this is, clients can do this on their own without help, any time some minor incident has been bugging them for too long. I use this technique myself, from time to time.

I remember one client, Chloe Clamup, a 30-something woman who suffered from bipolar disorder. We worked well together until one afternoon when she became moody and stopped talking.

Rick: "How are you doing?"

Chloe: (shrug)

Rick: "How was your week?"

Chloe: (shrug)

Rick: "What would you like to talk about this week?"

Chloe: (shrug)

No matter how I tried to draw her out, all I got was:

Chloe: (shrug)

This continued for *weeks*! I confess it was getting to me. Most Wednesday mornings, I would wake up with a headache. (Chloe's appointment was at 3 o'clock each Wednesday.) One Wednesday morning, I finally faced the fact that this was really bugging me and decided the VKD Lite technique might help.

I spent 5 minutes or so doing it. I turned her into a cartoon character with goofy circus music in the background.

At 3 o'clock, I sat with Chloe.

Rick: "How are you doing?"

Chloe: (shrug)

Rick: "If this isn't a good time for you, we can cut this short and try again next week."

(Why didn't I think of this weeks ago?)

Chloe: (Startled) "No. This is fine. I mean, this week is fine."

End of problem.

Once, I was asked to teach the VKD technique to our agency's entire adult outpatient staff. I began by demonstrating VKD Lite on a volunteer. My personal favorite choice of silly music for the VKD Lite technique is that stereotypical circus music we all know. ('Dat dat...dadadada... dat dat... dada...' ...you know the one.)

When I demonstrated the technique, I used that circus music as my silly music example. The class went well. I'm sure some clinicians adopted the VKD techniques, and some didn't.

But, the next time we had an Adult Outpatient team meeting, my fellow clinicians started humming and whistling that circus music when I walked into the room. It became a regular thing for a month or so.

I'm sure I was one of the few psychotherapists with his own theme song.

VKD Technique

The actual VKD technique for PTSD is more involved and requires a therapist's presence. Unlike the "Lite" version, there is no
silly music, no cartoon characters. I use completely different elements to help dissociate severe traumatic events. Psychological
safeties are in place. We're not shooting for giggles when treating
real trauma.

When a trauma client trusts me enough to be able to close his
eyes in my presence, I first ask him for a SUDS value from zero to
ten of just how upset he feels when he *briefly* recalls the trauma. I
have him relax and tell him that he is going to imagine himself
sitting in the back of a movie theater. What will appear on the
screen will be a brief, one minute film of his traumatic incident.
The film will run backward, from the point where the trauma was
over, to the point of safety, right before the trauma. In this brief
film, he sees all characters, including himself. I remind him that
he is in the back of the theater watching this film and then instruct the client to close his eyes and begin when he's ready. He is
to open his eyes slowly when the brief film is over.

I ask for a SUDS value again. Usually, it has decreased. I have the
client do this a few more times, if necessary. Each time, I add another dissociative element to the film. Possible elements include:

1) Make the film black & white
2) Make the film blurry
3) Reduce the size of the picture on the screen

4) Make the film an animated drawing

I have asked several clients with severe PTSD symptoms to imagine sitting in the back of the theater watching themselves sitting in the front of the theater watching the screen. This adds one more safety element.

It was common to see a PTSD victim's SUDS scale go from 10 to zero in a single session. When a client reported a SUDS value of one or zero, we were done. Some clients required a few sessions before they got there.

VKD was effective with combat vets. They didn't perceive it as girly, hippyish, or New Agey. I used it effectively with them as well as with sexual trauma clients. The caveat is that you must establish trust. You're asking this person to close his or her eyes in your presence. That is a huge challenge for someone who is guarded and hypervigilant. A PTSD victim doesn't want to close his or her eyes in *anyone's* presence, let alone be busy in their head while you are sitting four feet away.

During the month or so following the VKD session, clients reported how this symptom and that symptom had somehow disappeared, but it may take as long as six months before getting to that session. Trust is everything.

The Reality of Working with Trauma

*(There are some intense and potentially upsetting stories here.
Some of you may wish to skip this chapter.)*

Working with most anxiety disorders was always fun for me. I'd get to shake up and loosen up all these rigid, over-thinking, con-troller types. My biggest challenge was to get them to have fun and have a good laugh at themselves during their therapy. In a few short months, we were done, big hugs, and call me if I can ever be of help again.

Treating trauma is very different. I get to retain my personality, but the sessions aren't fun and playful, nor are they over in a few short months. What's worse, you get to know these clients well enough to care about them and have to deal with the reality of what happened to them.

I've never been a combat veteran, but I've listened to a man who was the only survivor of a bombed naval destroyer. He drifted in the ocean, clinging to a floating object for four days before he was rescued. "What are you supposed to do when every commanding officer above you is dead? No one was there to tell me what the fuck to do next. No one was there to say that help was coming." That's a hard story to hear. There is no answer to that question. You can only listen and imagine that reality.

One veteran Marine described being separated from his company in Vietnam and chased by Vietcong for three days and nights. No food. No sleep. No radio. No hope. Three days seems short until you hear his detailed account of this.

I won't forget the veteran whose father, in the middle of dinner, made the mistake of saying, "I know just how you feel." At those words, the veteran snapped. He shouted, "You know how I feel?" as he picked up his water glass and crushed it in his hand, severely cutting his hand in multiple places. He then squeezed the blood over the food in his plate shouting, "You know how I feel?" as he shoveled the bloody food into his mouth and ate it.

There was the guy whose father took him for a ride in the car when he was seven years old. His dad parked the car in a remote area, said goodbye to his son, then put a gun to his own head and fired.

I led a veteran's therapy group where a Vietnam veteran commented that WWII veterans were lucky to return home as heroes.

One WWII veteran spoke up. He served on a ship in the Pacific during WWII and revealed that, while most WWII veterans returned home to cheers and parades at the end of the war, his ship was reassigned to move from island to island killing stray Japanese soldiers and burying many alive in huge mass graves. This took more than a year to accomplish. By the time those veterans returned home, WWII was old news. There were no parades. No admission that our military had done such a thing. No account in the most thoroughly-researched histories. 50 years later, he still felt a crushing guilt over this. "Not all of us returned as 'heroes'."

I worked hard with an 82-year-old veteran who had earned five battle stars during WWII. To appreciate this, you should know there are US generals who never received five battle stars.

This little guy, Harvey, was trained as an Army weapons specialist. Every time he was sent to a new area, it would be the site of a major conflict, from fighting Field Marshall Rommel's army in North Africa to the invasion of Nazi Germany to participating in the Battle of the Bulge, the bloodiest battle of WWII. That's how battle stars are won. Each denotes that you fought in a specific battle where there was a high likelihood of getting killed.

I remember him describing his company's invasion of Nazi Germany. After one particular town had surrendered, he walked in on his commanding officer in the act of raping a 13-year old German girl inside a church. Harvey was ordered to leave and never speak of the incident. Later, the same commanding officer ordered the town burned to the ground. He told Harvey to use his flame-thrower to burn every last building to the ground. When Harvey reminded the officer that the townspeople had surrendered, he was asked if he was refusing to obey an order.

Harvey dutifully took his flamethrower and burned house after house.

Then he torched a horse stable. As it burned, he could hear the horses inside become agitated. Then, he heard them screaming. For 50 years after his experience in WWII, he had a recurring dream *each night* of those horses crying out. He even smelled them burning each night. He said it bothered him more than carrying and burying the bloody, bloated bodies of dead friends after the Battle of the Bulge.

When Harvey eventually returned home, he became a firefighter.

His PTSD was so severe that he slept with a loaded handgun under his pillow each night after returning from the war, even during the decades when his wife lay beside him. Whenever a war scene came on TV, Harvey would sit paralyzed, unable to move, with tears streaming down his cheeks.

He managed to stop drinking. Then, he abandoned the loaded handgun. Next, we worked on getting him to exit the room when war movies or scenes came on. He was concerned about what people would think if he left the room. I convinced him that re-injuring himself was much worse. This took more work than all of our previous goals.

Our PTSD veterans were particularly shaken up by the tragedy of 9/11. For them, it was as though "the war" had followed them home. Months afterward, someone at the state or federal level of the VA decided they could save money by terminating part-time staff. I never saw Harvey again.

There was the nurse whose mother-in-law was going to babysit her one-year-old son while the mother went to work. The mother-in-law had a psychotic break that morning. She entered the house and locked the door. She threatened the mom with a hammer and wound up hitting her head severely when the mom tried to take her baby and leave the house. Now the mom's head was bleeding all over her white nurse's uniform. The mother-in-law got a huge kitchen knife and kept the mom and baby prisoner from 8 o'clock to nearly 3 o'clock, the mom's head bleeding the whole time.

The mom managed to escape the house at around 3 o'clock. She went to a neighbor's and called the police. When the police came, she got her baby back, unharmed. She saw me because

1) She couldn't look at raw meat in the grocery store without vomiting.

2) She could no longer tolerate being intimate with her husband.

3) She felt guilty that she had escaped the house without her baby.

We managed to fix everything but the guilt.

I worked with countless rape and incest cases, but I'll just share two of them.

One young man had a diagnosis of bipolar disorder. He was in a day treatment program run by my agency. He had a feminine demeanor that caused most to assume he was gay. He was 26 years old and never had a job or a love interest.

When I met him, he said that something happened to him in the past that he couldn't discuss. He wouldn't even categorize it. After seeing him weekly for a few months, I used the VKD technique without even knowing what the nature of his trauma was.

We spent half of one session doing this. When we finished, he reported that his upset scale was a "1". He said, "Do you want me to tell you what happened? I can now. It won't bother me."

He proceeded to tell me that he had been raped by a male babysitter when he was 12. He had never told this to *anyone*.

When I was asked to teach the in-service class on the VKD technique, he heard about it and asked me if I would like him to help with my presentation by telling the other clinicians his story and showing how it didn't bother him to talk about it anymore. I thanked him for the offer but didn't take him up on it. Over the next year, he got a job, a truck, and a girlfriend, who would later become his wife.

The second case was Sally, a woman in her 40s. She had been through two physically, emotionally, and sexually abusive marriages. She was an alcoholic who hadn't held a job in nine years. She couldn't look at mirrors. She had none in her home. There was more to the case, but I'll keep this brief.

I helped her with some minor issues before tackling the mirrors. For this issue, the treatment I used was progressive desensitization over an extended period. Months later, she was doing funny voices pretending to be opera characters singing in front of the mirror, making herself laugh.

Soon afterward she told me that since she was six-years-old, her father would take her to the bathroom, make her drink alcohol, and sexually violate her in front of a mirror. He told her that this was the only way a man would ever want her. This continued regularly until she left the house when she was 19 years old. Throughout that time, Sally's mother was depressed and didn't want to hear any of Sally's accusations about her father. Sally was the only client who required nearly eight weeks of the VKD technique. I honestly wasn't sure it was going to work at all.

But it did, and she got better, stopped drinking, and got a job working for a major department store. She had a real flair for arts and crafts and began making and selling things. To this day, I still have Christmas ornaments she made for me as gifts. When I left that agency to move to Maine, she wrote me a five-page letter thanking me.

That's a small glimpse of what it's like to work with trauma. You get to know these people and get hit with the reality of what they've experienced. It's not as fun or fast as working with anxiety clients, but it's incredibly rewarding to help someone get their life back.

Treating PTSD requires lots of patience while you establish trust. It requires much compassion and sensitivity when the story begins to emerge. It requires the ability to leave your work at the office. Up to 25 percent of clinicians experience "secondary trauma" or "vicarious trauma". This occurs when one starts experiencing actual trauma symptoms from listening to and absorbing these traumatic stories. I've avoided this by always leaving work at the office. If a client's story bugs me, I step into a fellow clinician's office and vent. At the end of the day, I listen to fiction books on CDs in my car. Once home, I tell only the funny stories.

"DEPRESSED? ...JUST CHEER UP!"

"When you are the victim of depression, not only do you feel utterly helpless and abandoned by the world, you also know that very few people can understand, or even begin to believe, that life can be this painful." ~Giles Andreae

When I first enrolled in grad school, I imagined that I'd be pretty good at treating depression, since I suffered from depression as a teenager and understood the disease well. Once I was in actual practice, I discovered that the opposite was true. Despite a very clear understanding of depression and how it permeates one's thoughts and manipulates one's choices and actions, I found I had a tendency to push depressed clients a bit too hard. I helped lots of people with depression, but it would never be a specialty.

I would amaze my depressed clients by accurately putting a voice to their thought process, but I would expect results too soon – ironic for the guy who was so patient with traumatized clients.

As I used to tell my supervisors, "If I was *perfect,* you couldn't afford me!"

Depressive disorders come in many flavors such as Major Depression, Dysthymic Disorder, Seasonal Affective Disorder, Psychotic Depression, Postpartum Depression, etc.

I recall my depression as a time when I saw the world through shit-colored glasses. I only saw the pain, the losses, the disappointments, and the negativity in this world. I found ways to discredit and disregard anything positive. I was a victim. Everything happened outside my control. Nothing I could do would possibly make any difference. Everyone but me knew exactly what to do and say. They had "the manual" and I didn't. I was the square peg in a world full of round holes. I would never fit. I would never belong. I would never matter. I only took up space and used up resources. That was my reality.

Today, in contrast, I'm one of the happiest and luckiest people I know, and I got here without anti-depressant medication.

The best way to understand depression is to understand that there is a "voice" inside your head that doesn't belong there. That's a strange concept because we assume we have only one voice in our head: Our own.

But while your voice advocates for *you*, the voice of your depression advocates only for itself.

> *Your depression ultimately wants you dead. And the only way it can achieve that is by separating you from the two things that make life worth living: People and Activity.*

It accomplishes this by having you make your decisions based on what you *feel like* or *don't feel like* as if you were four years old.

Mom: "Eat your cauliflower."

4-year-old: "I don't like it!"

Mom: "You haven't **tried** it."

4-year-old: "I don't **like** it!"

Children aren't talking about the *taste;* they are saying that just the look of this strange thing on the plate is enough to tell them they want nothing to do with it. It's *yucky*. Just *look* at it! Four-year-olds base every decision on feelings.

Try asking four-year-olds if they would like an ice cream cone *now*, or *two* ice cream cones 30 minutes from now. Who cares if you offer *ten* in 30 minutes? "Gimme my ice cream!!"

Now ask *me* if I'd like $1000 today or $2000 tomorrow. I'm likely to ask if I get $3000 if I wait until the day *after* tomorrow. That's the adult brain kicking in. That's also the difference between making decisions based on one's *thinking* vs *feelings*.

Friend: "Hey! A bunch of us are going out tonight. You should come. It'll be fun!"

Depressed person: "Nah. I don't feel like going out. Maybe next time." (The voice of your depression never *feels like* doing *anything*.)

Later that evening, you're lying on the couch with a pint of ice cream and a spoon, half-watching whatever is on TV, and mostly listening to your inner dialog.

Voice of depression: "See what a loser you are? Your friends are out having fun, and you're stuffing your face, watching some stupid shit on TV."

The irony is the same voice that said you didn't *feel like* going out is now the one making you feel bad about that decision.

The voice of your depression exists to make your depression worse. The more you base your decisions on that voice, the worse your depression gets, so it's vital that you learn to distinguish that voice from your own. Bear in mind that voice needs to separate you from people and activity, and it will do that by reviving your inner four-year-old. Everything strikes you as yucky. You don't want to do this or that because you *know* you'll have a bad time. You'll choose to stay home and feel awful about yourself and your decisions.

So what's the answer? I've already given you the best answer: learn to distinguish the inner voice that advocates for *you* from the inner voice that advocates for *your depression*. I'll offer a few more strategies. Follow them or don't. I promise not to push you too hard. Heck, I'm a *book*! What can I do?

140

Your first instinct will be to choose with your feelings, so we need to force your brain into having a vote.

1) Choose people and activity.

2) Ask yourself, "Which choice will make me feel better about myself?" Your depression will push for what will most erode your self-esteem. Guaranteed.

3) Imagine what you'd like your life to be like five years from now. Better yet, write it out. Then, when you have any decision to make, ask yourself, "Which decision will get me one step closer to the direction I want to move in?"

4) There is such a thing as a "depressed lifestyle". It includes staying up late and getting up late, watching lots of television, social isolation, neglected hygiene, and lack of exercise. Not only does depression bring on a depressed lifestyle, but living a depressed lifestyle can bring on depression. It's one of the reasons we see so many retirees and people with temporary disabilities become depressed. Do the opposite. Change your sleep habits. Sneak some exercise into your day, even if it's just taking walks. Turn off the TV or computer and read a book instead.

5) To combat the lack of motivation that accompanies depression, I recommend making an ongoing list of things that you *need* to do (e.g., trip to the post office, pay monthly bills, make Dr's appt, etc.) Next, add to that some things that you would *like* to do (e.g., take a walk, visit friends, try a yoga class, etc.) The next step is to commit to crossing a number of them off that list per day. Some of my depressed clients have found this helpful because, while pushing themselves to get things done, they see themselves moving forward and taking control.

Severe depressives benefit from medication. I've treated suicidal clients who couldn't do this work until medication took some of the "edge" off, allowing them to concentrate.

Suicide

Here are some interesting things I've learned about suicide.

1) Someone who sincerely wants to be dead will succeed. No warning, no cry for help, no suicide note, and a slim chance of failure or being prematurely discovered. It's a harsh reality.

2) People feel suicidal when their pain exceeds their perceived capacity to cope with the pain.

3) In a study among people who survived drastic falls in suicide attempts, 70% admitted they regretted jumping while on their way down. I call this the "Oh Shit! Response."

4) 70% is also the percentage of suicides in the U.S. that happen under the influence of alcohol or drugs.

5) Most people who are suicidal convince themselves that the world (including their family and friends) will be better off without them. I'm quick to point out how, if you commit suicide, there is a one in three chance that one of your children will follow your example. After all, it's what mom or dad did when stressed to the limit. Even your grandchildren will have a higher likelihood of suicide than the general public. This is a valuable fact to share with suicidal patients/clients who, typically, don't want to hurt anyone and convince themselves that the world will be

better off in their absence. I also tell them about the clients we've seen in counseling whose mental health issues began with the suicide of a loved one.

6) The number of deaths by suicide has increased yearly. It is now the tenth leading cause of death worldwide.

7) In the US, twice as many females suffer from depression as men. Women make three times more suicide attempts than men. But men account for 80% of suicides while women account for 20%.

8) In the U.S., the three leading methods of suicide are by firearms: 51%, suffocation (hanging): 24%, and poison: 16%. Worldwide, the figures are hanging: 50+%, pesticide poisoning: 30%, while firearm suicides rank 3rd.

9) In the US, the suicide rate is 19% among people 45 to 64 years old, 19% 85 years and older, and 11% in 15 to 24 year-olds.

10) 80% -90% of adolescents that seek treatment for depression are treated successfully using therapy and/or medication.

I consider myself fortunate that none of my depressed or bipolar clients ever successfully committed suicide, only attempts and threats, and cries for help. When I think of suicide, the most memorable case that comes to my mind was that of Jack.

Jack and his estranged wife had two children. Jack was a 27-year old alcoholic with depression who had tried committing suicide by plunging a knife into his stomach. Jack was hospitalized for the wound and then transferred to a mental hospital. Before he was released, the hospital set him up with me to treat his depression on an outpatient basis.

First, I encouraged Jack to quit drinking. Then we revived his interest in activities and hobbies he once enjoyed. Jack had many strained relationships in his life. He no longer spoke to his father, his sister, or his estranged wife. One by one, we managed to help him heal each of those relationships. After several months of treatment, Jack was doing great. I couldn't have been happier.

Jack's appointment was always on Monday at 5 PM. One evening, he didn't show up. Being late was so unlike him. I was concerned. I called his house around 5:30. His mom answered the phone. When I told her who I was, she said, "Jack was found dead on Saturday morning. I'm sorry, I can't talk right now." Then she hung up. I was crushed! Jack had been doing so well. How could he have possibly committed suicide at this point in his life?

When I left the office at 7 PM, my friend and colleague, Claire, asked if I was okay. I explained the situation to her and told her I was upset. Claire said, "There was a reason he got you as his therapist. You helped him tie up all of those loose ends." I thought about that during the drive home. Thinking about that helped, but I still couldn't understand his suicide.

A few days later, I got a call from Jack's mom.

"I'm sorry I couldn't talk with you more on Monday. We're all devastated. Do you remember that Jack stabbed himself three months ago, before you and he met? It turned out he punctured the bottom of his lung and the hospital never saw it. That put a strain on his heart this whole time. Friday night he watched a movie on TV with his dad, then went to bed and died of a heart attack in his sleep."

"I wanted to thank you for all you did for Jack. You made his last few months worth living and I got my son back."

Don't tell any of my former employers, but I would have done this work for free.

OTHER ASSORTED NUTS

There are plenty of good detailed books available covering all mental illnesses and conditions. Rather than make this book encyclopedic, I'll share my take on a handful of them.

Bipolar Disorder

I remember learning that bipolar disorder (formerly known as *manic-depression*) was a strictly biological disease. Something in the brain chemistry causes this disorder, so the right dose of the right mood stabilizer will balance it. The client will be completely healthy, like giving insulin to a diabetic.

My experience suggested otherwise. There *is* evidence that bipolar disorder runs in families, but why were so many of my bipolar clients also sexual trauma victims? I don't have the answer, but I suspect it's not as simple as a glitch in the brain chemistry.

It *is* true that once on the right dose of the right medication, bipolar clients can live relatively normal lives. But, it's not as simple as that. In my experience, people with bipolar disorder are the least medication-compliant people on the planet. It's a funny thing. I've yet to meet a diabetic whose blood sugar level was so stable he decided he didn't need insulin anymore.

But people with bipolar disorder who finally find the right dose of the right mood stabilizer drug seem to wake up one morning and notice how good they feel and decide they no longer have a mental health issue and, therefore, they no longer need medication.

They don't *really* think that, but it sure seems like it.

First, it's important to understand bipolar disorder. Imagine that we have a range of emotions. Let's say that the happiest we get is on our wedding day or the day our child is born or on the day we win the lottery. On a scale of 1 to 10, that day is a 10. On the other end of that scale is losing a dear loved one, a parent or a child. Let's call that sadness and grief a zero. So, our normal emotional range is zero to ten.

It's different for bipolar clients. They have no such limits. When they are in the depressed cycle of their illness, their mood can drop to 10 below zero. In their manic phase, their high can soar to 20 or more. The depressed phase is hard to distinguish from major depression, but the manic phase is – interesting.

The manic period begins with a feeling of well-being. Imagine being a happy person without having to do any inner work. Euphoria without drugs. But, as they become *more* manic, they might begin talking faster or jumping from one random idea to the next. They might become restless and take on new projects. They might become impulsive and engage in high-risk behaviors. George Eliot called this, "Feeling dangerously well." The manic phase can be so severe in some bipolar clients that they can become temporarily psychotic.

Some fun examples of the manic phase would include the guy who drove his car along Boston's Southeast Expressway at 120 MPH late at night until his car died in front of the Callahan Tunnel. He stripped off all of his clothes, stood on the roof of his car, and yelled his political and religious opinions to any drivers approaching the tunnel.

Let's not forget the dad who woke up and decided it was a perfect time to remodel the living room. He got a sledgehammer from the garage and, at 3 o'clock in the morning, began smashing down the wall between the living room and the dining room.

Less humorous was 18-year-old "Rufus the Kid," who, during his manic phase, decided he could rob the local liquor store with nothing but a finger poked into his jacket pocket. (Even the most outlandish ideas sound perfectly reasonable to someone in their manic phase.) The liquor store owner probably suspected the young man didn't have a gun but, the store owner *did* have a gun.

He took his gun from under the counter, pointed it at the young man, and told him to leave and never come back again. Now, most of us would leave and thank the heavens to be walking away from such a stupid scheme but, not our manic 18-year-old. He got the idea that he could reach across the counter, grab the gun, and shoot the store owner before the store owner could shoot *him*.

That's exactly what he did. He shot and killed the store owner and served the next 13 years of his life in prison – for a manic episode.

He became my client upon his release when he was 31 years old. Medication-compliance continued to be an issue.

He eventually stopped taking his mood-stabilizer and began taking herbal supplements. One day, during his appointment with his female psychiatrist, he stripped off his clothes and invited her to meet "The *REAL* Rufus!"

He was hospitalized. I never saw him again.

One young woman I worked with was easily my most intelligent and engaging client ever. She turned me onto many authors, movies, and TV shows. She would get stabilized, stop taking medication, and become destabilized. Then she would stop showing up for her appointments so that I wouldn't see her becoming manic and be disappointed in her. It was her dream to become a teacher. She would have been a good one. I could imagine her teaching a college class and having everyone engrossed.

She finally landed a teaching position and was so happy she stopped taking her meds. Soon, she had a meltdown in front of her class, yelling and pulling out her hair. It marked the end of her brief teaching career as well as the end of her med-compliance issue.

What many bipolar clients have admitted to me is that when their mood becomes stable, they miss the feeling of extreme well-being that comes in the early half of the manic phase.

So what can we clinicians do for bipolar clients? Three things: help them with their med compliance, help them manage their emotions, and help them feel less crazy, less defective.

Using that young lady as an example; she was a voracious reader. When her extended family got together for a cookout or gathering, she preferred to sit by herself and read. Her family's response was a whispered, "It's her mental illness." Her boyfriend was critical of most everything she did, even the way she dressed. One focus of our work together was getting her to understand that she was allowed to have a personality. It was even acceptable to be quirky. I often reminded her, "Not every aspect of your personality is the result of your bipolar disorder." I did my best to convince her that the right guy would love her just the way she was and not waste so much time and effort trying to rebuild her into the girlfriend he really wanted. (She later found such a guy.) She also found another career she enjoyed. Today, she spends lots of her free time reading, writing, and honing her artistic skills.

I have several personal friends with bipolar disorder. One of them stopped taking his meds and, three days later, decided to get a motel room and hang himself. But first, he thought he should stop and say goodbye to me.

I was still a Human Resource Director – not a therapist yet – just his friend. I spent the next six hours trying to talk him out of it. I'm happy to say that he is still alive today. When I got accepted into grad school, he asked me what made me decide to switch careers and become a therapist. I said, "I want to be able to talk someone out of suicide in under six hours next time."

Schizophrenia

The layman should know, schizophrenia is not multiple personality disorder ("split personality.")

It never was.

Schizophrenia is a permanent psychotic condition. It's the mother of all mental illness. It comes on, usually without much warning, usually between the ages of 16 to 25. Approximately 1 percent of the world's population is schizophrenic. No one knows why.

There are five types of schizophrenia: Paranoid, Catatonic, Disorganized, Residual, and Undifferentiated. Paranoid schizophrenia is the most common.

Symptoms of schizophrenia are divided into two categories: positive and negative. Positive symptoms are things that shouldn't be there: hallucinations, delusions, disorganized behavior, and disorganized speech. Negative symptoms are things that are missing: emotional expression, motivation, social skills, self-care, etc.

Paranoid schizophrenics often seem to live in an entirely different reality than the rest of us. They perceive things differently, based on elaborate belief systems created in their minds.

To offer insight into the mind of the schizophrenic, I'll share a story.

Trudy Transformer was one of my mental hospital patients. Her biggest complaint was that now and then while she slept, someone would remove her head and replace it with someone else's. She told me she had been Betty Crocker, Fannie Farmer, Winston Churchill, Elizabeth Montgomery, Jesus Christ, Aunt Jemima, and others. She said she had ten children and was forced to watch a video where the Mafia skinned one of her children alive.

Schizophrenics don't lie.

Think about the wildest dream you ever had. Mine was one where I could fly without a plane. I remember every detail. I remember how to climb, how to dive, how to bank left or right. But I've never flown without a plane.

How can I possibly remember something that never happened? The experience originated in my subconscious. Fortunately, I woke up and said, "Whew! What a cool dream!"

Now imagine if your subconscious planted false memories *when you weren't sleeping,* memories you couldn't discount as dreams.

Welcome to the world of schizophrenic delusions. Trudy *remembers* waking up and looking in the mirror and seeing Aunt Jemima looking back at her. She *remembers* watching her one of her ten children skinned alive. She *remembers* having had ten children. (She only had one. He was alive and well and living in foster care.)

Schizophrenics don't lie. They have false memories and experiences mixed in with the real ones.

Anti-psychotic medications can make the delusions and the hallucinations stop, but they don't erase the memories, nor do they much effect on the negative symptoms of schizophrenia.

With patience, you can teach personal hygiene skills and social skills. You can teach someone to take a bus and hold a job. Once you have won their trust, you can even use my dream analogy and explain about the random stuff that comes from the unconscious. Then, you can teach them to look objectively at their own memories and ask themselves "Is this likely?", and "Does this happen to other people?"

It's quite gratifying to hear a schizophrenic tell you, "I remember that happening, but I don't think it really happened."

It's hard to fake schizophrenia. It's too pervasive. I did a memorable agency intake on a guy, Peter Putz, who, before I could even ask a single question, handed me a piece of paper. Written on the paper were these words: "Depression, PTSD, paranoid skitzofrenia."

Rick: "What's this?"

Peter: "That's what's wrong with me."

Rick: "Okay. Tell me about your depression."

Peter: "That means I'm depressed."

Rick: "I know what it means. I'm asking exactly how you experience this depression."

Peter: "It means that I'm sad all the time."

Rick: (pause) "Okay. How about PTSD?"

Peter: "You don't know what that means?"

Rick: "Why don't you tell me."

Peter: "It's like depression."

Rick: "(sigh) Okay. How about 'paranoid schizophrenia'?"

Peter: "That means I'm paranoid."

Rick: "And tell me what *that* means."

Peter: "That means I think that people are after me."

Rick: "And *are* they?"

Peter: "*Of course not! ...I just think they are.*"

<Groan>

That's the sort of story my wife hears when I get home. In case you're curious, Pete was alcoholic with a case-of-beer-per-day habit. He was hoping to be declared eligible for permanent disability (free beer). A friend wrote that piece of paper for Pete and assured him that it would work. He was diagnosed alcohol dependent, given an appointment with our alcohol counselor, and never seen again.

Snappy Habib was a Muslim client with delusional disorder. Think of that as "schizophrenia lite." It's a rare condition where the person has bizarre delusions but not enough symptoms to warrant a diagnosis of schizophrenia or schizoaffective disorder.

Snappy's wardrobe probably cost more than my car. He wore his pants so tight if he farted it would have blown his shoes off. His sports car probably cost more than my house. The other clients in our waiting room probably thought he was a pharmaceutical salesman — or a male prostitute.

Snap was convinced that invisible "evil spirits" followed him at all times. He was always aware of their presence and their intention to do him harm. He even shared a detailed description of the three distinct types of evil spirits that persecuted him. He was un-willing to consider medication.

Apparently a girlfriend insisted he accompany her to see a for-tune teller. Snap believed that the fortune teller disliked him and put a curse on him, resulting in these evil spirits. He was immov-able in this belief. This was his reality.

Time for a creative intervention. I asked him who had power over these evil spirits. He said that only Allah did. I asked how we could enlist Allah's aid. He said that he believed that there were prayers that could help. I asked if these were prayers that he knew. He said that only priests at the mosques would know the proper prayers. His assignment was to travel to the nearest mosque, which was about an hour's drive, and inquire about prayers to cast out evil spirits.

That did the trick. The last time I saw Snappy all he had to report was that the evil spirits were gone. His entire presence was trans-formed. It was like James Bond pulling up in his Aston-Martin to tell me that we had thwarted the bad guys and saved the day.

Do I believe that praying to Allah had banished his evil spirits? Of course not. My belief system said that he was delusional. But working within *his* belief system held the key.

When I was an intern at the state hospital, I worked with as many as ten schizophrenic patients at a time. Once I was working for community mental health agencies, I established a few bound-aries. I would be willing to take on one borderline personality disordered client at a time and one schizophrenic client at a time. Both require very hard work.

I was once asked by my agency to take on a 21-year old schizophrenic client whose former therapist refused to work with him after he purchased a large knife for the purpose of "gutting" her. He refused to take any medication. I agreed to meet with him.

Now, instead of goofy circus music when I walked into our weekly clinicians' meetings, it was "Eeeeek... Eeeeek... Eeeeek!!!" from the movie, "Psycho." Now I had a theme song and a soundtrack.

During my first meeting with the client, Sweeney Gutter, I said, "I agree to work with you on the condition that if you should ever get it into your head that you want to gut *me*, or hurt me in any way, you'll tell me immediately."

He agreed.

He was a nice kid. He later agreed to take haloperidol (Haldol) any time his symptoms became unmanageable. Haldol is effective in treating acute psychosis. Mental hospitals often use it when patients are out of control. It tended to calm Sweeney down quickly and put him to sleep for the next day or two. When he awoke, he said it was as if someone hit a "reset" button. However, neither I nor his psychiatrist could convince him to take anti-psychotic meds regularly.

Sweeney's biggest problem was the constant voices in his head. Those voices told him to gut his last therapist. He found that he could control the voices somewhat if he yelled at them. But people tend to get a bit uncomfortable around anyone who yells at imagined voices. We successfully managed to suppress his tendency to yell at the voices when people were around. I taught him transcendental meditation, having no idea whether it would be effective, or even possible for a schizophrenic. He said it quieted the voices for a while.

Sweeney was lucky enough to land a job mowing a golf course. He did this first thing in the morning before the golf course opened. He was able to yell at the voices all he wanted since there was no one to see or hear him out on the fairway. I wished that he would take anti-psychotic medication on a regular basis and just shut off those voices, but he found his own particular way to manage them.

One of my more sadly persecuted schizophrenia clients was Tim. Tim was in his early 60s when I worked with him. He believed that everyone could read his mind. Anytime Tim heard someone laugh; he was convinced that they were laughing at his thoughts. If he was in my office and heard someone laugh in the waiting room, 40 feet and several walls away, they were laughing at him. If he heard anyone clear their throat, it meant that they weren't pleased with his last thought. Every week, when Tim had to shop for groceries, as soon as he walked into the supermarket, he knew everyone in the store was monitoring his thoughts. I wish I could tell you that I was able to offer him some degree of relief from this, but I was not.

While schizophrenics live in their own personal reality made up of random ideas and false memories, there is also one interesting, inexplicable phenomenon I have observed more than once. From time to time, a schizophrenic has accurately reported something he or she couldn't possibly know.

Tim told me about his fear of ambulances. He hated hearing their sirens. He said that he would someday die in an ambulance.

A year later, Tim had a heart attack. He died in the ambulance on the way to the hospital.

Stranger still was the case of Roger Rasputin. During my internship at the state hospital, I sat with a bunch of paranoid schizophrenic patients from one of the men's wards. One particular guy was interesting. He asked if I had ever read a book on Yoga by Swami Vishnudevananda.

That was the *only* book on Yoga I had ever read. It wasn't even a very famous book. Weird coincidence.

Then he said to me, "So. The one son. Is that your only child?"

How would he know I had a baby boy? I didn't share that sort of information with patients. I didn't even wear my wedding ring at the hospital. Lisa, one of the nurses, overheard and asked me if I had a son. I said I did. Lisa said that this same guy told her that her birthday was on June 5th. It was on June 6th. I turned to him and asked, "How would you know that?" He shrugged and said, "I just know some things."

Several months later, Dr. Ahmed told me that there was a schizophrenic in one of the locked wards who was ready for individual therapy who requested to be assigned to me specifically. This was a first. We couldn't imagine why a patient I didn't know would ask for me, but I agreed to meet him.

Imagine my surprise when it turned out to be Roger Rasputin, my psychic acquaintance. I took him on as a patient, and we worked well together. About three months later, he was ready to go home. His brother was scheduled to pick him up later that afternoon. We walked around the hospital grounds, summarizing our work together. Just before our session was over, I said, "Do you remember the time when we first met, and you told me I had a son?"

Roger: "How would I know that?"

Rick: "That's what I was going to ask you! You told Lisa that her birthday was June 5th, and it was on June 6th."

Roger: "How would I know that, Rick? I don't remember saying anything like that."

Was a dormant part of his brain opened up when he was ill? Had his medications shut it down? Why didn't he remember any of it? Strange stuff.

Borderline Personality Disorder

I don't plan to discuss all of the personality disorders. They were never my thing, so I have few insights to share. But I did get to work with lots of people with borderline personality disorder (BPD), mainly because lots of clinicians dislike working with them.

If schizophrenia is the mother of all mental illness, then BPD is the mother of all personality disorders. It's the only one that allows its victims occasional visitations to Crazyville.

Remember the movie, "Fatal Attraction"? In the beginning, Glenn Close's character is intelligent, attractive, seductive, and soon she was boiling the kid's pet bunny. That's the borderline: seductive at first and temporarily psychotic when she feels abandoned in any way.

Borderline clients are difficult to deal with, especially if you are a member of the opposite sex. Female borderlines have a tendency to prefer male therapists because they feel they can more easily manipulate them. The female borderline tends to behave seductively with her male therapist. She does her best to make him feel special. "You're the best therapist I've ever had! You understand me so much better than my psychiatrist does!"

Of course, her psychiatrist hears all about how *he* understands her so much better than *you* do! This is called "splitting." Borderlines assume that none of us compares notes.

Borderline clients will often try to find as much personal information on you as they can. They want to know where you live, which car is yours, your marital status, your history, your phone number, etc. At one time, they would routinely look for you in the phone book. Today, a simple internet search yields lots more personal info.

Borderlines have no emotional self-regulation. Their anger becomes rage. Their sadness looks like deep depression. Any feeling of abandonment can trigger a violent and even psychotic response. Borderline clients are extremely manipulative and often use suicidal gestures and threats to manipulate others.

One thing a therapist must *not* do with a borderline client is to compliment their appearance in any way. If I was to compliment a female borderline on her hairstyle or her clothing or her attractiveness, I might as well suggest we get a motel room. That's what she'll hear. You have to set firm boundaries with borderline clients.

Dialectical Behavior Therapy (DBT) groups are most effective for the treatment of borderline clients. DBT is a treatment that uses a combination of cognitive, behavioral, and mindfulness elements. Clients are taught to use specific actions and skills to combat specific symptoms.

For example, whenever depressed clients told me that they missed last week's session because they were too depressed and couldn't get out of bed, my immediate question was, "Did staying home in bed make you feel less depressed?" Of course, the response was: "No. I got more depressed."

Rick: "Why would you do something that made you more depressed? Wouldn't it make more sense to do something that made you *less* depressed? What else could you have done?"

This is the same logic behind DBT: When you feel *this*, do *that*.

I once had a borderline client named Vivian Vixen, who never kept a boyfriend for more than a week or two.

Vivian was in her mid-20s. She wasn't particularly attractive, but she had a peculiar way of moving her mouth when she talked with me. It never failed to grab my attention. I always found myself focused on and fascinated with how she moved her mouth. She never did this when she talked with our female support staff.

Vivian finally met a boyfriend who lasted a whole two months with her. One evening, her boyfriend was watching a movie with two male friends. Vivian was in another room. A very voluptuous woman came on the screen. The three young guys began excitedly commenting on the actress's breasts.

In walked Vivian. She stood in front of the television.

"I thought you told me you didn't like big breasted women?" She caused a loud scene in front of her boyfriend's friends. Later that week, the boyfriend decided he wanted nothing more to do with her. He asked her over to his house. They went upstairs to his bedroom where he sat her down and gave her "the talk".

"It's not you; it's me. I'm just not ready for a relationship. You deserve much better than me."

You know, "The talk."

Vivian was very understanding. "Okay. I'm just gonna go."

He walked her to the stairs. She let him go first. As soon as he was on the stairs, she grabbed the railing and kicked his back with all of her strength. The poor guy went tumbling down the stairs and landed flat on his face. Vivian walked calmly down the stairs, right over his back, and out the front door.

Can you understand why many clinicians dislike working with borderline clients? Vivian and I shared the same birthday. I joked with fellow clinicians that it was absolute proof that astrology was just baloney.

Before we leave the subject of seductive clients, I'll offer one more example. I once had a married client who described in detail her sadism/ masochism escapades with her husband. She would "bleed" her husband with a linoleum knife as a preamble to sex. (I remember thinking how pain would have just the *opposite* effect on *my* erection!) The most ironic part was her complaint that her husband was a "control freak" outside the bedroom. Then she went on to describe various affairs she had enjoyed with her various doctors and therapists.

(Hmmm...)

The following week, she showed up wearing a see-through blouse, under which was a fairly transparent bra. The outfit left nothing to the imagination. I was reminded that she made it a point to tell me she had many affairs with her health care providers. I was also reminded of what her idea of sex was. I focused my attention on her face for the whole hour.

The third week she came in dressed like a kindergarten teacher. I never saw her again after that. She ran off to Florida with her latest lover.

I once worked with a borderline male client named Carlos Cutter. Male borderlines are rarer than females. Carlos was seriously into self-mutilating behaviors. His self-cutting had been under control for months.

One day he showed up in our waiting room with 17 safety pins going through the skin on his left arm. Carlos showed his arm to one of my other clients, who was waiting to see his psychiatrist, and said, "Wait until Rick sees *this!* He'll freak!"

My other client said, "Nah. Rick won't even be surprised." (He told me this the next time I saw him.)

When it was time for Carlos's appointment, he sat in front of me with his arm in plain view.

"What's with your arm?" I asked curiously.

"17 safety pins" Carlos proudly announced.

"Wanna talk about it?" I asked calmly.

Sure, I was grossed out, but I wasn't going to let a borderline manipulate a reaction out of me. For the rest of the time I worked with him, Carlos still had other serious problems, but he stopped self-mutilating.

Before I leave the subject of personality disorders, A less-successful case of mine was Sarah Burnheart who wanted treatment for "depression."

Sarah had no depressive symptoms. What she *did* have was a histrionic personality. She was what you might call a "drama queen." I suspect she complained of being depressed hoping to get some quality attention from her neglectful husband.

One evening Sarah came to my office, completely decked out and manicured, as always. She talked about everything except her feelings. She ignored every attempt I made to bring the conversation around to anything relevant.

Finally, without warning, she grabbed both my hands and cried, "I want to go to God!" and proceeded to lie down on my office floor, full-length leather coat and all, still holding both my hands.

Awkward.

She just lay there, relaxed, with her eyes closed. She wasn't crying. She was just lying there holding my hands tight. It forced me to sit on the edge of my seat. Waiting.

...and waiting.

The thought crossed my mind that I could lie down beside her and say, "So. How long have you been feeling like this?" or "Excuse me. Is this part of the floor taken?" or "Hi there! Come here often?"

I amuse myself in awkward moments like these.

She eventually opened her eyes and got up off the floor, perfectly fine and composed. I'm sure she had expected more fanfare or an ambulance or something. She never returned.

Substance Abuse

"We gain the strength of the temptation we resist."
~Ralph Waldo Emerson

During my first few years in practice, I hated doing substance abuse counseling. I would convince someone to quit drinking or drugging or whatever. I'd set them up with detox, if necessary, and a 12-step group to supplement the individual therapy. They would get clean and sober, get a decent job, get their first pay-check and spend it on drugs or alcohol.

I found it frustrating. Clients I helped with anxiety, depression or trauma never backslid. I never had a client complain that she missed having panic attacks. But, I would work much harder with an alcoholic for months and months just to see it be for nothing.

At least, that's how it felt.

Then one day I ran into a guy I had treated several years earlier. He had been one of those who got sober, relapsed and stopped coming to therapy.

I asked how he was doing, and he said he had been sober for over a year. When I congratulated him, he said he had me to thank. That seemed unlikely until he explained that something I said made a huge impact on him. (Sorry, I don't remember what it was I said or this would be the perfect place to share it!) Even after he relapsed and stopped making appointments, whatever I said kept going through his mind and eventually inspired him to get sober again.

The therapist in the office next to mine was a recovered alcoholic. He wasn't a bit surprised when I told him the story. He said, "Substance abuse is a disease of relapse. Of those who eventually succeed, many relapse a bunch of times in the process. Something you said planted a seed. That seed took root and grew."

It changed my attitude. I no longer saw relapses as utter failures. I saw the counseling as "planting seeds," knowing that my efforts might or might not take root and grow someday.

The more I worked with substance abuse cases, the more I saw the similarity to my former cigarette addiction.

20 years ago, I smoked three packs of cigarettes a day. That's two cartons a week. One day, while driving in the car with my four-year-old son, he announced that he was going to smoke cigarettes when he.grew up.

Now this child once wanted to wear his blue and white striped shirt to an event because dad was wearing a blue and white striped shirt. He was a "mini-me" in those years, and he saw me light a cigarette every 15 minutes. It was time to quit.

Most people you know who have quit smoking cigarettes smoked an average of one pack per day. That's only *playing* with cigarettes! I smoked 60 cigarettes a day. When a heavy smoker like myself quits smoking, his whole body freaks out.

My chronic cough got much worse; my 20-minute visits to the toilet were replaced by 20-second "power-dumps", and my well-managed temper gained a hair-trigger.

I knew that quitting would be a challenge, so I enrolled in a smoke cessation class that my agency offered. They taught us lots of behavioral tricks like sucking on plastic drinking straws cut to cigarette-length, putting all ashtrays out of sight, getting up from the table as soon as you're done eating, relaxing in a different chair, munching carrot sticks or sucking on hard candies while driving, and continuing to take time out for breaks, only without smoking.

Nicotine patches had just hit the market around the time I quit. The trouble was, the strongest patch sold is the equivalent of smoking seven cigarettes per day. To someone who smokes 60 cigarettes a day, that's about as satisfying as smelling a smoker's breath. The patches were no help at all. The behavioral tricks did help.

Before I quit, I warned my wife that, when I couldn't stand it any longer, I would probably disappear into the bedroom and read.

It was hard, but I did it.

Quitting smoking gave me insight into what my alcohol and drug-addicted clients went through. I understood the habit and the thought process.

One of the potential minefields in addiction recovery is that people give themselves permission to relapse. "I've been clean and sober for six months now. Doing it just this one time won't hurt." One can even interpret the motto, "One day at a time" to mean "I stayed sober today. I may not tomorrow. It depends on how stressed I am." Relapse remains a viable option.

The best thing I did was promise myself that I wouldn't smoke again, no matter what. The smoking option was off the table. I would say to myself, "I'm dying to have a cigarette but I'm not going to do a thing about it." or "The smell of cigarettes makes me miss smoking, but I'll never smoke another cigarette again."

20 years later, I still haven't smoked a cigarette.

No chapter on addictions would be complete without my take on methadone programs. In the early days, U.S. methadone programs were government sponsored. They determined how much methadone your heroin addiction warranted, dispensed that much, then soon began tapering your dosage until you were completely weaned off of opioids.

Then came the "third party providers," who saw the opportunity to profit. Federal and state agencies were more than happy to farm out their methadone services. The third party providers determined how much methadone your heroin addiction warranted, dispensed that much, but neglected to taper addicts off of the methadone. After all, they weren't in business to get addicts *clean;* they were in it to sell methadone.

I've had clients who *asked* that their dosage be reduced. They were sent to a "counselor" who had neither a license nor, in some cases, a college degree. They warned clients that reducing their dosage would be a grave mistake. They told horror stories of addicts who relapsed on heroin as a result of tapering their methadone dosage. Legally, they couldn't *refuse* to taper their dosage, but they could change their minds.

It was all very sleazy.

One heroin addict I treated was a truck driver who lost his license, his wife and his home because of his addiction. He wanted desperately to get back on his feet. I would encourage him to ask his program to systematically reduce his dosage, and they would scare him into changing his mind. Finally, he insisted, and the tapering process began. The last time I heard from him, he called me from New York. He was driving an 18-wheeler to Florida.

One of the dubious "benefits" of any addiction (alcohol, drugs, nicotine, food, sex, etc.) is it keeps our negative emotions in check. You've heard the term "self-medicate." Most addicts I've met use their addiction to keep their sadness, anxiety, or anger at bay. When you stop feeding your addiction, those emotions come blasting through the floodgate.

Feeling is Healing: The Truth about Emotions

Emotions are our most healthy and natural method of coping. Picture two 18-month old babies stacking blocks. Suddenly both of their beautiful towers collapse. One baby reacts by crying while the other gets angry and kicks the blocks. Two different reactions but, in a minute or two, both babies are joyfully stacking blocks again.

Their emotions helped them get past the tragedy of the fallen tower. It's the purpose of our emotions.

Think about toddlers. How many times have you seen a toddler run and fall and immediately start crying? He isn't hurt. The fall scared him. We check him for injuries. We hug him and console him. Abruptly, he stops crying and is off and running again.

If babies and toddlers thought like some adults, many of them would decide they have no inherent talent for stacking blocks or running and never try it again. When adults repress emotions, that energy gets transferred to that hamster wheel in our head where it becomes unresolvable guilt, anxiety, self-doubt, or even self-loathing.

Many cultures are uncomfortable with emotions. Here, in the US, sadness is not traditionally considered masculine. Anger is not considered feminine. Fear indicates weakness. It's okay to be happy, but too much expression of joy makes people uncomfortable.

On the other hand, look at the Italians.

It's not uncommon to see Italians wringing their hands with grief over some small thing, or two Italians arguing, yelling at one another, making hand gestures, even poking and gently back-handing one another in apparent disgust, then going off to enjoy some wine together.

Some cultures get it right.

When we see a widow crying at her husband's funeral, we don't worry that she'll require mental health hospitalization. We know that the crying is part of a healthy grieving process. But there are doctors who medicate adults with fluoxetine or diazepam to "get them through" emotional events such as these.

Emotions are healthy. Granted, they can go wrong. The bipolar person in their manic phase can be *too* happy. The person with depression is sad while grieving no loss. The person with anxiety disorders experiences paralyzing fear when there is no imminent threat. How many people use anger as an excuse to hurt others?

We commonly think of ourselves as passive emotional receptors, like human thermometers helplessly reacting emotionally to the world around us. We imagine our emotions to be the natural response to everything that goes on in our world, every event that happens, every word that's spoken. The problem with this is it creates a victim mentality. I can be emotionally injured by anything and everything around me. A stranger may say something insensitive to me, and I'm crushed. I might feel devastated by minor disappointments.

An emotionally-healthy adult can change his or her mood. There comes a time when we have been sad, frustrated, worried, or angry long enough. We need to be able to recognize when it's time to change gears, and we need to have a ready arsenal of thoughts and activities that allow us to do just that.

There will always be pain and loss and disappointment, but joy and love and beauty is always within our reach. They were there all along, but you have to make a conscious step toward them. You need to figure out what activities, people, and thoughts make you happy and deliberately include them in your life.

Insulting words do not define me. This or that disappointment, seen in the context of my entire life, is probably not as devastating as it feels right now. Perhaps it's time to see friends or go dancing, hiking, bowling, gardening or whatever turns my mood around. One of my favorite mood-changers is group drumming. I get to turn off my head and be in a state of bliss for a time. Your mood-change arsenal will be different than mine, but it's vital that you have one and learn when and how to use it.

We need to be receptive to our emotions like we were when we were toddlers, but we also need the ability to brush ourselves off and get back to playing the way we used to.

Anger is the trickiest of our emotions. Many of us express anger poorly. I can express anger with you without attacking you physically or emotionally. Well-placed anger can sometimes effectively alter the situation that made you angry in the first place. I'm so good at writing angry letters; I often get refunds, free products, and apologies for my efforts.

With anger, the first question our adult brain must ask is, "Is this something I can change?" If the answer is yes, then what steps can I take to change it? If the answer is no, then how can I safely *feel and express* my anger, so that I can move on?

You and I are planning a fishing trip tomorrow. We've been planning this for months. We wake up to a torrential downpour. I'm devastated! I've been so looking forward to this. (Though, why I would be looking forward to a *fishing trip* is beyond me. It sounds as dull as playing golf, but sitting still!)

Do I kick over all the furniture and start smashing things? Do I run outside and do a rain dance? Or do I express how much *this sucks* and suggest we play some cards instead?

Anger is the one emotion we can express destructively.

You Wanna Talk *ANGER?*

"Holding on to anger is like grasping a hot coal with the intent of throwing it at someone else; you are the one who gets burned."
~Buddha

There are many books out there detailing cognitive and behavioral anger management strategies. I'll share a few stories you won't find elsewhere.

Some people think that therapists must hear the same stories again and again. While we may hear *similar* stories on certain topics, people have never failed to surprise me.

While working for the VA, I ran an anger management group for combat veterans with PTSD. I would typically ask new group members to describe their anger at its worst. Men described shouting and hitting and breaking things, nothing very surprising until it was Norman Nitro's turn to answer.

"Last week, I had a fight with my old lady (wife) over some shit. I forgot what it was about. She was pissing me off, so I pushed her down to the floor and pissed on her."

"You *pissed* on her??"

"Yeah, I pissed on her. She was being a bitch!"

(I wanted to ask, "...And you're still *married??*")

As it turned out, Norman's wife had an anger problem of her own, though, I can't imagine what she could be angry about, with such a loving and demonstrative husband. Each night, after our anger management group, Norman would share with his wife whatever we discussed in the group as well as the printed materials that I passed out. It was pretty cool that they worked on their anger issues together.

PTSD is responsible for some of the "road rage" that you hear about. One Vietnam vet that I worked with individually had a very respectable, high-profile job but had a serious road rage problem.

My client, Dave Deathmobile, would be driving along when some innocent woman would unwittingly cut him off in traffic. We've all done it. You pull out and *then* realize that you just cut someone off. You give an apologetic wave and show them your "I'm-so-embarrassed face" and drive away feeling like a putz for the next few seconds.

Only Dave took it personally. Dave would follow that woman, convinced that she saw him and did that on purpose. He'd be driving dangerously close behind her, getting himself all worked up, praying that his baseball bat was still in his trunk. There were a few times when he pulled right into someone's driveway, ready for a confrontation.

Fortunately, no one had been hurt or pressed charges – yet.

I tried teaching Dave every anger management technique I knew, all of the standards. Nothing worked. He just wouldn't or couldn't do them.

One afternoon, mostly out of frustration, I shared a personal story with Dave. I told Dave how I used to get angry with incompetent cashiers and waiters and salespeople until I realized that I was giving them power over me. I would always come away upset from the encounter.

Upset over a stranger? I'll probably never see this idiot again, and I'm stopping to have this big encounter with them? For *what*?

Wouldn't it make more sense to deal with incompetent people in a way that preserves *my mood*? If I get upset or argumentative, I lose. If I come away amused, I win. I have no control over the butthead on the other side of the counter, but I *can* control my reaction to his or her buttheadedness.

I've been doing this for years. I told Dave a whole bunch of stories, as examples:

Salesperson #1: "Can I help you with anything?"

Rick: "No thanks. I'm fine."

Salesperson #2: "Can I help you?

Rick: "No thanks. I'm fine."

Salesperson #3: "Can I help you find something?"

Rick: "An uninterrupted shopping experience?"

Telemarketer: "Is Judy there?"

Rick: "May I ask who's calling?"

Telemarketer: "This is a Courtesy Call."

Rick: "We get half a dozen 'courtesy calls' a day. The courteous thing to do would be not to call in the first place."

Cashier: "That's $12.43 out of $20.00. How would you like your change?"

Rick: "What are my choices?"

Cashier: "That's $1.50 out of $10.00. How would you like your change?"

Rick: "In cash, please."

Cashier: "Did you find everything you were looking for?"

Rick: "I found stuff you couldn't *pay* me to eat!"

Cashier: "Did you find everything you were looking for?"

Rick: "No. Some of the things I'm looking for are only sold in other stores."

Cashier: "Did you find everything all right?"

Rick: "I wasn't really shopping for *everything*."

At McDonald's:

Rick: "Could I have extra salt and ketchup?"

Counter person: "How many packets of ketchup and salt would you like?"

Rick: "I'll have three packets of ketchup and two packets of salt. No, make that two ketchups and three salts... Or maybe just a handful of each. Let's go wild!"

At Wendy's Drive-Thru:

Rick: "A large chili, please."

Speaker: "Would you like cheese with that?"

Rick: "Is it free?"

Speaker: "No."

Rick: "Same answer."

Those are fun but then I told Dave my favorite. It was 9:30 PM. The store closed at 10. I went in and grabbed some things I needed and headed to the cash registers. There were two, Register 1 and Register 2. Both register lights were out, and no cashier was in sight, so it wasn't obvious which one was open. I spotted an employee in her early 20s staring out the window in front of the store. "Excuse me," I said politely. "Which register should I go to?"

"I can see you at #1," she snapped as though annoyed by my asking. I headed to register #1 and put my purchases on the counter.

She lifted and scanned each article and tossed each one carelessly on the counter. She snapped, "$16.50" and, when I handed her my credit card, she blew air through her teeth like a tire deflating. Even my using a credit card pissed her off. After she had run my credit card through her register, she tossed it back at me. It bounced off the rubber conveyor.

When I picked up my bag, I leaned in really close to her. I said, "You know all those people who told you that you would be really good working with the public? ...They were making fun of you."

Then I turned and left the store, my back to her all the way so she wouldn't see the huge grin on my face. When I got into my car, I laughed out loud – all the way home.

I only told Dave these stories because I didn't know have any more techniques to teach him except to share my personal anger management strategy and a laugh.

But, some weeks later, Dave came into my office grinning.

"A woman pulled right out in front of me at Walmart. I did what you said, and it worked like a charm!"

I honestly had no idea what he was talking about. Had he finally tried one of the anger management tricks I had taught him months earlier?

"What did you do?" I asked.

"I waved to her with a big smile on my face. All the time I was mumbling under my breath, 'Look at you, you stupid bitch! You're looking at me, trying to figure out who I am with that stupid fucking look on your face! Look at that stupid face. Yeah, bitch. That's it. Drive away so I don't have to see that face anymore.'

"All this time, I'm waving at her and grinning, and the bitch is trying to figure out where she knows me from. You were right! I laughed for the next few blocks!"

He laughed. He didn't get upset and follow her. While making *him* laugh, I had unintentionally taught him a trick that worked.

One anger management lesson that could have backfired involved another combat veteran. Violent Vinnie used to get so worked up arguing with his wife that he would beat her with his fists. He didn't want to do this anymore and didn't know how to stop. We tried a few strategies that failed until I talked him into walking away at the first sign of anger.

I suggested that he find something physical to do. Go running; exercise. Walk away and then do something physical to try to channel that anger.

Vinnie agreed to try.

One day he and his wife started arguing over something. Just as the argument began getting heated, Vinnie stopped cold. His wife saw him walk through the French doors and out to his backyard, where he grabbed his huge ax! Imagine what must have gone through his poor wife's mind seeing Violent Vinnie pick up an ax in the middle of an argument.

But next, he picked up a piece of firewood and **BLAM**, exploded it in two with his ax. Vinnie proceeded to split nearly half a cord of firewood before coming back into the house and apologizing to his wife.

Back in the 1960s, groovy therapists used Bataka (foam) bats to treat anger and aggression. The theory was that having repressed anger was like being emotionally constipated. It all had to come out for you to feel better. You would see your therapist once a week, and you would both have these big foam bats and pretend to beat the metaphoric shit out of one another.

What no one considered was that how you express your anger becomes a habit. There is a real, emotional high one gets from the indiscriminate release of anger. Learning to hit *people*, when angry, is a lesson of dubious value. Better to take it from Vinnie and do something constructive like chopping wood.

First, ask yourself if this infuriating thing is something you can change or something you must accept.

Cruise Control

"Between stimulus and response there is a space. In that space is our power to choose our response. In our response lies our growth and our freedom." ~Viktor E. Frankl

There are three major differences between you and me. Three things that make *you* who you are and *me* who I am: Genetics, Nurturance, and Choices.

Genetics has determined my height and my hair and skin color, my resistance or susceptibility to some illnesses and conditions, etc. Nothing too profound here and not much I can do about it.

Nurturance is a bigger deal. How I was raised determines much of my personality, tastes, habits, joys, neuroses, and fears. A huge part of who we are was formed during our childhood.

As a result, many of us grow up blaming our parents and our childhood for our baggage. And, while it may be true that our baggage *originated* in our childhood, it avoids the question of why we still drag it around as adults.

That brings us to *Choices*. During our childhood and teen years, we began to have choices independent of our parents. We made good choices and bad. We learned from them, paid the consequences of those choices, or enjoyed the benefits of them.

When we become adults, no one tells us that we can choose to re-make ourselves. Most of us approach life with the belief that we are the result of our upbringing, for better or worse. It's convenient because my flaws and poor choices become someone else's fault. If I'm shy or overbearing or quick to anger, it was how I was raised. Deal with it.

I call this *"cruise control."*

Cruise control is who I am by default, the person my upbringing created, the person who is still reacting to my childhood experiences, reacting out of habit, the person who is still trying to please mommy or daddy or rebel against them. If I put no effort or thought into the way I interact, I'm in cruise control.

We don't have to be.

We can make adult choices that result in the type of person we want to be. We can make choices based on what sort of person, friend, worker, spouse, or parent we would *choose* to be.

I'll give you a personal example. As a dad, my father was marginal. He worked every day and put food on the table, but I have no childhood memories of him talking with me or playing with me. Ever. He took no interest whatsoever in anything going on in our lives. He just worked in a factory, drank a few beers at the VFW, came home, and lived in a private bubble. Spending time with my dad meant sitting in the same room with him while he watched a ball game on TV. And be invisible. Don't talk, even during commercials.

When my son was old enough to play with toys, he would say, "Daddy, wanna play cars?" The first thought that automatically came to my mind was, "Why in the hell would I want to get down on the floor and play with stupid little Matchbox cars?" That was my cruise control. That was the voice of my dad, the voice of my childhood.

But I didn't want to be my dad. I was determined to be a better husband and father than he was. I couldn't change my father or my childhood, but *I could be the sort of father that my son deserved.*

How would *that* father have responded?

The response my son grew up with was, "Sure, Buddy!"

I got down on the floor and chose a tiny car. At first, this felt silly and awkward. As a child, I pretty much played alone. My brother was ten years older than me. Before long, the awkwardness faded, and I was engaged in playing with my son.

> ## My son grew up with the dad I chose to be, not the one I was trained to be.

As for my dad, I learned that his father had been an abusive alcoholic. My dad's bubble was for *his* emotional protection. It was for keeping him safe, not keeping us out. It also kept him from becoming abusive. He refused to be like his dad.

Just like I refuse to live in a bubble.

All of our neurotic behaviors happen in cruise control, without thought or intention. We need to train ourselves to delay those automatic reactions long enough to ask ourselves, "What sort of spouse/ parent/ sibling/ friend/ professional/ employee/person do I *want* to be? Can I react in a way that makes me feel *good* about myself?"

We can be whatever kind of person we choose to be. We just have to begin making conscious choices. It's hard at first. Cruise control kicks in automatically and feels as natural as breathing. Cruise control is comfortable because we don't have to question our own actions or their consequences. Expect to catch yourself screwing up just *after* you've done it. When that happens often enough, you may start catching yourself *while* you are screwing up. Your ultimate goal is to catch yourself *before* you screw up.

Your life and the person you are is the result of every choice you have ever made. When we learn to slow our reactions and ask ourselves what sort of people we would *choose* to be and start making choices with that in mind, we can create our healthy adulthood.

"Live as if you were living a second time, and as though you had acted wrongly the first time." ~Viktor E. Frankl

RELATIONSHIPS: SEA-WORTHY OR SINKING?

What Goes Wrong In Some Relationships?

People often are confused about why a relationship often starts out great and then just sort of falls apart, inexplicably. Here's what I've learned:

When we first meet, our relationship is superficial. We talk about the weather, the books we've read, the movies, food and music we like, all relatively safe topics. As we find things in common, we begin to feel a bit closer. Not what anyone would consider a deep relationship but we're enjoying each other's company, and there is hope.

As we get closer and move to the second level of deepening, we might begin to discuss religion, politics, morality, ethics, etc. Here, we may hit a snag. I'm liberal, and you're conservative. You're Jewish, and I'm Christian.

Here's the thing about snags: some we manage to work through, and some we don't. For instance, my wife was Catholic, and I was raised Catholic and became Unitarian Universalist at age 18. It was no big deal. We had a Catholic wedding but personalized it Unitarian-style. Win-win. For some people, dating someone of a different religion would be a deal breaker. That's neither right nor wrong. It's just important to understand.

All snags that surface as a relationship deepens can be worked through, suffered, compromised, or they become deal-breakers.

When we encounter a deal-breaker, the relationship stops deepening. Period. It has gone as far as it's going to go. Either we end the relationship, or it remains a superficial friendship at whatever level the deepening process stopped.

The boyfriend you're so excited about admits that he just got out of jail for child molesting. I'll bet many women would consider that a deal-breaker. Any abuse, physical or emotional, should be considered a deal-breaker, despite the fact that so many people tolerate it.

Which brings us to the next level of deepening in the relationship: revealing yourself. We share stories of our childhoods, our past relationships (romantic, family, friends, etc.), our past mistakes, and regrets. Here is a virtual minefield of possible snags. Sex falls into this level of intimacy also. Some snags you'll get through easily, but any one of them might be a deal-breaker.

The best thing about the relationship deepening is that we feel more deeply accepted and loved as our relationship deepens. If we have come this far and still have a relationship, great. The next minefield is the biggest: emotional compatibility.

The first time we argue about something, what will it look like? Will it be a mature discussion? Will one of us lose our temper? Will there be blaming? Name-calling? Cursing? Will it become physical? Abusive? When you see me after a bad day and need to talk or be held, do I care? Am I interested in listening? "Sorry. I'm heading out with the guys. Why don't you call your mother or one of your girlfriends?"

Sometimes, one partner becomes so close, emotionally, that the other partner abruptly backs away because he or she is not capable of, or interested in that degree of emotional intimacy.

Emotional compatibility is more important than most people understand. Here is where couples most often get it wrong. "Our love will get us through anything!" "I'll domesticate him." "I'll make her jealous." "Things will change once we're married." "Things will change once we have a baby."

We're so ignorant about emotions and personalities that we don't understand that some partners are compatible with us emotionally, and some never will be. And this is the deepening phase that will continue the longest time. If you've learned to work through snags pretty well, or have learned to compromise*, then you might make it through this phase and wind up with a healthy, loving relationship and a partner for life.

That's the simple answer. Want the more complex answer? (Here comes a snag.)

People change.

The partner who once couldn't keep their hands off of you becomes disinterested in intimacy. Your once fun-loving spouse becomes a couch potato. These are snags, too. We either work through them, suffer them, find a compromise, or they become deal breakers, and we reconsider the relationship.

* Remember that compromise results in a win-win situation. It is not the same as giving up pieces of yourself or what you want or need.

Abusive Relationships

"Where love rules, there is no will to power; and where power predominates, there love is lacking." ~Carl Jung

Abuse can occur between any two people and can take the form of physical assault, psychological manipulation, damage to one's self-esteem, humiliation, verbal mistreatment, or sexual assault. Abusers can be men or women. I'll share some of what I've learned in the hope that it might help an abuse victim.

The longer you put up with abuse, the harder it is to walk away.

When I work with abused women, my job is to convince them that the abuser won't change, and all she can do is *get out*. It's not an easy thing for her to accept. Her self-esteem is at rock bottom. Deep down, she doesn't believe she deserves better than this. She's afraid that no one else will ever love her. She's afraid of what her partner might do if she should leave. She wants to believe his excuses. She wants to believe that their love is so special that it will somehow get them through this.

No abuser starts abusing on the first date.

First, he must win you over. Then, he must wear down your self-esteem. No one with a healthy sense of self-esteem allows abuse. The most effective and least detectable way to lower self-esteem is to poke fun of some weakness or mistake. He does it in the spirit of "only kidding" or teasing but it becomes a running joke that subtly affects you, makes you feel defective, less lovable. Abusers usually have control issues, so the abuser now begins "correcting," in the guise of helping or teaching you something. Correcting soon becomes criticizing and adds to the further deterioration of your self-esteem.

People with controlling personalities unconsciously enjoy the superior feeling that they get from correcting and criticizing others but pretending to teach or tease minimizes the chance of negative consequences.

I should make it clear that most people with controlling personalities are *not* abusive, but most abusers have controlling personalities. Some abusers suffer from antisocial personality disorder and narcissistic personality disorder.

The mental health field has an abysmal record of "fixing" abusers.

That's because controlling another person is a deeply-seated need for controllers. The act of abusing becomes a primary source of the perpetrator's self-esteem and gratification. Domestic violence offenders are often forced by the courts into mental health counseling, but they simply learn to say whatever will satisfy the counselor. It's important to understand that the abuser feels guilty of no wrongdoing.

Another factor that prevents change is that losing one's temper becomes a habit. It's like a drug. It is a great feeling of release — a rush – for the person who is losing his temper. Once you give yourself permission to express rage against another human being and get away with it, no one can take it away.

Blaming is a common aspect of abuse.

Abusers take no responsibility for any of their wrong actions. They see every abusive act as a natural response to something their victim did, failed to do, said, or failed to say. Catch an abuser with his hand in the proverbial cookie jar and he'll tell you he was *forced* to do it because *you* didn't give him any cookies. All abusers want you to believe that you can stop the abuse by changing *yourself.*

How many women have told me that their spouse "warned" them that, if they said "one more word," he wouldn't be responsible for the outcome? Then, of course, the abused spouse says something and gets hit and tells me how it was, ultimately, *her fault* because he warned her.

Bullshit! There is *nothing* my wife could say to me, nothing my wife could do to me that would make me hit her or be emotionally abusive to her. She could get me to walk away. That's all.

Other common aspects of abuse are manipulation and guilt. Abuse victims eventually reach the point where they want and *need* the approval and love of their abusers. This is often a huge factor in why they stay and tolerate the abuse. Abusers are motivated solely by their own self-interests. If you want to know why an abuser said or did *anything*, ask yourself how it benefited *him.* Abusers are incapable of loving another person in any meaningful way. But they are experts at using their victim's need for attention and affection to manipulate them.

It's important to understand that, while abusers are incapable of loving others, they're incapable of loving themselves, also.

Abusers need to feel superior.

They will obsessively find fault, teach, correct and criticize.

There is an unspoken agreement in every successful, healthy relationship: *"I'm not perfect, and you're not perfect. I'll live with your imperfections if you can live with mine. I prefer to go through this life with you."*

In an unhealthy relationship with control issues, the unspoken attitude is, "Here is *perfect* (hand held high) and here is *you* (hand held low). I'm going to devote my time and energy to pointing out the difference."

Abusers often grew up with an abusive parent.

If Dad hit or attacked emotionally when he was angry, then a child learns that it's a normal expression of anger. Emotionally-healthy men learn the opposite lesson.

If you are in an abusive relationship, and you have kids, your kids are learning two lessons:

Being abusive is normal.

Tolerating abuse is normal.

Abusers often isolate their victims.

He doesn't like your friends and family and does his best to sever or weaken your ties with them. He has worked very hard to get you under his control. An objective friend or relative who genuinely cares about you might see right through his game and ruin things for him.

Abusers apologize to minimize consequences.

It's inconvenient to have to charm and train a new victim. Here is the "Cycle of Abuse":

a) *Tension building phase*

This occurs prior to an overtly abusive act and is characterized by poor communication, passive aggression, rising interpersonal tension, and fear on the part of the victim. During this stage the victim may attempt to modify his or her behavior ("walking on eggshells") to avoid triggering their partner's outburst.

b) *Acting-out phase*

Characterized by outbursts of abusive, sometimes violent, incidents. During this stage, the abuser attempts to dominate his or her partner, with the use of physical or emotional violence. This is the most destructive and hurtful part of the cycle.

c) Reconciliation phase

Characterized by affection, apology, or ignoring the incident. This phase marks what appears to be the end of the abuse, with assurances that it will never happen again, or that the abuser will do his or her best to change. During this stage, the abuser expresses feelings of remorse and sadness to minimize the possibility of consequences for his actions. Some abusers walk away from the situation with little comment, but many will shower the partner with love and affection. Some abusers may threaten self-harm to gain sympathy and prevent the partner from leaving the relationship. Abusers are frequently so convincing, and victims are so eager for the relationship to improve, that victims will stay in the relationship.

Although it is easy to see the outbursts of the Acting-Out Phase as abuse, even the more pleasant behaviors of the Reconciliation phase perpetuate the abuse because the victim is now convinced that the relationship isn't all bad, convinced that there is hope, and the abuser has successfully avoided any consequences for his actions.

This phase usually ends with a period of relative calm and peace before interpersonal difficulties inevitably arise, leading again to the tension building phase*.

---

* Some experts break the Cycle of Abuse down into as many as eight distinct parts. I prefer to help fix anal-retentiveness rather than practice it.

Abusers don't abuse consciously.

They abuse *automatically*, which is worse. Where there is a conscious effort, there can be a conscious choice to stop. Automatic behaviors are not a matter of choice. The last breath you took was not a conscious choice. Abusers abuse as thoughtlessly as they breathe.

Like all controlling personalities, the abuser has little insight. He believes that his abuse is a perfectly normal reaction to his victim's behavior.

While the abuser robs his victim's self-esteem, he gains a huge dose of self-esteem from abusing. Apart from the satisfying rush he gets from losing his temper, the abuser feels *clever and powerful* when he manipulates his victim. In many cases, this is the only situation in the abuser's life where he *does* feel clever or powerful.

Many abuse victims protect their abusive partners.

They do this by helping keep his ugly little secret. They often feel embarrassed to admit they're in an abusive situation. It's important to understand that when they keep abusive behavior a secret, the abuser wins. He stays in control. Victims need to confide in trusted friends and relatives. Tell them what is going on. In the long run, it's an insurance policy. The abuser is limited as to how he can hurt you and what he can get away with when there are people in your life who know what's going on.

There are women's shelters in many areas that will work with abuse victims and help them to leave quietly and without incident. It's worth looking into. It costs nothing to talk with people who understand and are there to help.

Why Do I Keep Choosing The Worst Possible Partner?

Until you make the unconscious conscious, it will direct your life, and you will call it fate. ~Carl Jung

By the time you've worked with hundreds of couples, you start seeing common patterns. Here's the big one:

Many of us take the most difficult relationship of our childhood ...and we marry it!

Ever wonder why so many children of alcoholics marry alcoholics? Ever wonder why so many abuse victims marry abusers? The numbers would shock you.

If you had a parent who was emotionally unavailable, or controlling, or anti-social, or non-supportive, there is a good chance that you fell in love with someone who shared that same negative quality.

Why? Because we get a sense of familiarity with potential partners who share that quality which we experience as sexual desire or "chemistry". That familiarity feels both attractive and comfortable. It's how children of alcoholics are attracted to alcoholics before they even know they have a drinking problem. It's why people with a physically or emotionally abusive parent will be attracted to an abuser long before the abuse begins.

It's also one of the reasons that so many first marriages fail. We unknowingly drag the worst of our childhood into our adulthood. Some believe that there is an unconscious desire to heal or fix the most painful relationship of our childhood.

I've known people who have married the same type of person four and five times and still can't figure out why each of their marriages failed.

Of course, we're not aware that we are doing this. All we feel, initially, is the magnetic attraction. But, as the relationship continues, our partner is eased into the role of surrogate mom or surrogate dad. We unconsciously set them up so that we can say to them what we wish we had said to our difficult parent or so that we can continue to play the role (caregiver, mediator, martyr, teacher, challenger, victim, etc.) we played in our childhood.

So, what's the answer?

List the worst qualities of your mother, father, and older siblings. Next, list your partner's or ex-partner's worst qualities. Make the same list for former partners from past long-term relationships. Do any of the negative qualities of your romantic interests match those of your family? Those match-ups are the qualities you want to consciously *avoid* the next time.

Want to take it one step further? List the best qualities of your parents. The ones you valued most. Add to that list the qualities you *wish* had been in your family: more humor? Stability? Affection? Playfulness? What was missing? Now you have a list of qualities you are going to look for in a partner. No one may have them *all*, but you'll be looking for what you *need* and *want* in your life instead of constantly winding up with the same toxic character again and again.

I had a female client whose abusive boyfriend had pressed her pregnant body against an anchor fence with his pickup truck. At 24-years-old, she had five kids, all from a long string of abusive boyfriends.

In case you're curious, she had an abusive mom.

After I had helped her get out of this relationship, she met a nice guy who fell in love with her. She was *uncomfortable* dealing with someone who treated her lovingly. This was a first for her. She came to me one week and said, "He bought me *flowers!* I didn't know what to say. Why do you suppose he did that?"

One time, she fell behind paying a utility bill. She owed $200 she didn't have. Her new boyfriend offered to give her the money. She refused. Then he offered to loan her the money. She came to me for advice. She said, "I can't help but feel like, if I take the money from him, he's going to expect something in return."

I said, "What if he doesn't? What if he's offering it because he honestly cares about you?" That idea was preposterous to her. "No way does anyone care about *me* without wanting something." I suggested a test.

"Let him loan you the money. If his attitude changes and he expects something in return, then we'll know that you were right. I'll help you dump him. But if it turns out that he offered to help because he really loves you, he passed the test. Either way, you'll have learned something valuable."

He passed this test and many others. My client finally relaxed and, for the first time, fell in love with a guy who adored her. They married and moved to Florida, five kids and all. I got a Xmas card from her every year letting me know how happy she was.

When you figure out who will keep you miserable, you can begin to recognize who might make you happy.

How Do I Know If He or She Loves Me?

How many times have we heard this question asked? Hundreds of questions boil down to this one. Believe it or not, there *is* an answer.

When we're in a relationship, I can lie about how I feel and what I think. "I love you so much! You're so special to me. I wouldn't want to live without you. I so look forward to our life together. I've never felt this way about *anyone* before! You're my soul mate. We were meant to be together. You're in my heart 24/7. I think about you all day. I even dream about you at night!"

Words are easy. Even abusive partners use words (after the abuse) to keep their victims on the hook, to keep them hopeful and forgiving. "I don't know what got into me. You know I'd never do anything to hurt you! I promise it'll never happen again."

But this isn't just about abusive relationships. This is about defining Love as a feeling, like joy or indigestion, and making big declarations expressing love. It proves nothing. Users, abusers, and losers can all use words that sound sincere.

So how can you tell how someone *really* feels about you?

Love is how you treat someone.

I can spout loving words until the day I die, but I can only treat you lovingly for so long. When I feel secure in our relationship, I'm going to relax and how I treat you will begin to reflect how I really feel about you.

Do I listen to you? Do I enjoy spending time with you? Do I treat you with respect? Am I present for you, emotionally? Am I supportive? Do I go out of my way to make you feel loved? It's easy to tell you that you're special. Do I *treat* you as if you were special? Do I treat you lovingly?

I can fake it for a short time, that honeymoon period when we are trying to meet each other's expectations, but eventually I'm going to let my guard down and let my true feelings slip out. If you're very lucky, I'll continue to treat you lovingly. If I'm very lucky, I'll get that back from you in return.

But, many of us begin taking each other for granted as soon as we feel secure in the relationship, and many of us accept it because we want to believe the loving words and refuse to consider the unloving behavior.

Love is how you treat someone.

It's the only accurate test of someone's feelings. How does she treat me once we're "comfortable"? Does she prefer spending time with friends than with me? Am I nothing more than an interruption while she is focused on her computer/ phone/ TV/video game? Am I expected to do whatever she needs and then be invisible afterward with no needs of my own?

Does he or she come home and pick a fight after a bad day at work? I call this being an "emotional toilet" when someone uses you to dump their crap. I don't mean coming home and sharing one's stressors so that you can be supportive. I mean coming home and provoking an argument so that they can have the fight they couldn't have elsewhere, using you as a safe place to dump their anger.

Does she use me to play out her control issues? Does she play "teacher"? Does she constantly find reasons to criticize? To correct? Does she put me down so that she can feel superior?
I'm not talking about the occasional slip. We all make mistakes. I'm suggesting paying attention to trends and patterns.

Love is how you treat someone.

If you ever want to know how someone feels about you, pay attention to how they *treat* you. There lies the truth.

Relationship Counseling Cases

The same Relationship Counseling professor who psychoanalyzed me in front of the class showed us a memorable video series of her doing counseling with a young couple.

The couple had no babysitter available so they would bring their one-year-old son to their couples counseling sessions.

In the first video, the wife complained about her husband. He was an unemployed cook who wasn't making an effort to find a job. Their finances were strained, especially with the baby. The therapist kept asking the husband to address these complaints, but he would just sit there hunched over, looking shameful, and not say a word. The hour-long session was spent listening to the wife complain.

Our professor asked for a show of hands. "Who is at fault, here?" Eight out of ten of us sided with the wife. One woman and I insisted that we needed more information. We needed to hear the husband's side of the story. Classmates argued that he had been given the opportunity to defend himself and didn't take it. We contended that, until we heard from him, we didn't know the whole story.

In a later episode of the video series, the one-year-old son, fell down and cried. He immediately ran to his dad. That struck me as strange. Babies gravitate to their mothers. What was going on here?

In another episode, the son began to cry. The husband said that he was probably hungry. The wife took the big bag of baby supplies and rifled through it. She turned to the husband and asked, "Where's his bottle?" The husband reached into the bag and pulled the bottle right out.

By the time we reached the end of the video series, we had learned that the husband had been offered a job cooking for a desirable restaurant. The wife had insisted he pass it up because it would require her to stay home with the baby each evening and she liked to get dressed up and go out nightclubbing while the husband stayed home with the baby.

Why hadn't the husband defended himself? He loved his wife. He didn't want to fight. He didn't want to suggest that she was a liar or a less-than-perfect mom.

We don't know the whole story until we know the whole story. Nor can you choose sides based on gender or who complains the loudest.

Well into my practice, I got my most interesting couples counseling case.

Barney and Betty were both 40 years old. They were an average-looking couple who had been successfully married since graduating from high school. They enjoyed bowling together. Their married lives had been happy and uneventful.

Betty's complaint was that Barney had become suspicious of her. He was always questioning her about her whereabouts. He had been rifling through her pocketbook on a regular basis. The last straw was when she discovered that he had been tapping their phone and recording her conversations. They had separated the day before their first appointment with me.

I asked to see Betty alone the next week and then Barney the following week. During the week I saw Betty, it was clear that she was as deeply in love with her husband as she was back in high school. She had recently taken up country dancing. Barney uncharacteristically refused to participate. She wound up dancing with whatever partner was available. She was shocked and disappointed that he had suddenly become so distant and distrustful of her, after all those years.

My session with Barney held the key. He was deeply in love with Betty, who stuttered since childhood. When she turned 40, her stutter disappeared. As a result, she became more confident and out-going. She made a complete personality change, and this was when he became suspicious. He couldn't explain why. He had no evidence of infidelity.

I told him about Gestalt Therapy and the "Empty Chair Technique." I told him that I would put an empty chair in front of him and ask him to pretend that Betty was in that chair and say what he wanted to say to her. Then, he would be asked to switch chairs and answer for Betty.

I warned him that this would be uncomfortable and awkward but assured him that it was the best way I knew to get to the bottom of this and fix this quickly (They had been separated for two weeks by now.) He agreed to try it.

I would quote the whole conversation verbatim, if I could, after all these years. Instead, I'll share the basic idea of it. Bear in mind that Barney was speaking both parts:

Barney: "I know that you're cheating on me."

Betty: "Why would you think that?"

Barney: "Because all of a sudden you're so happy. Your whole personality has changed, and it's not because of *me!*"

Betty: "It's because I stopped stuttering. You know how much I hated stuttering and how happy I am that it stopped."

Barney: "What I know is that you wouldn't have looked at me twice back in high school if it wasn't for your stuttering. You were too beautiful for someone like me. The only reason you liked me was because I was nice to you. I didn't make fun of you like some of the others. *That's how I won you!* But, you don't need me anymore. You're *perfect* now. Now you can have anyone you want. That's why you're out dancing."

At this point, Barney stopped. He remembered how hard Betty had tried to convince him to take up country dancing with her. He realized that, deep down, he believed that she was only with him because she had been flawed. Without that flaw, she didn't need him anymore. She could find someone better.

He admitted that didn't sound like her at all. *This was his fear talking – his insecurity – not his wife.*

Our next session was with both of them. They were already back together again. He enrolled in her country dance class. We talked about Barney's revelation. The two of them cried and hugged a lot.

Betty and Barney were responsible for a half-dozen more couples who asked to see me for counseling, over the next few years – some who knew them from bowling and some from dancing.

The Key to Successful Relationships

People commonly think that the secret to a great relationship is communication, but it isn't. It's Compatibility.

I can prove it. Imagine a couple that wakes up in the morning, shares a kiss, eats breakfast quietly while each reads a novel or newspaper, kisses goodbye, goes to work, returns home, eats dinner, watches TV, shares a goodnight kiss and goes to bed. (The kisses are optional.) They have done very little communicating because neither of them is very talkative. But they both value stability and companionship, and they love one another. I wouldn't want my marriage to be so bland. But they are Compatible. Not with me and maybe not with you, but they are perfect for each other.

Verbal communication is unimportant except for those of us who value verbal communication. Compatibility is the key. When you argue that communication is the key to a happy marriage, you imply that the couple above is not successfully married, and I say that they are.

Compatibility is one of the least-considered issues behind every successful and unsuccessful relationship. Some couples have sex twice a day while others haven't had sex in 10+ years. Neither of these extremes is a problem until someone who wants sex daily marries someone who thinks once every ten years is plenty.

We often fail to consider compatibility when choosing a partner. We become intimate with someone who has several qualities that we enjoy and assume everything else will just fall into place or work itself out. Then we find ourselves committed to someone who wants to stay home every night while we want to go out. Or someone who likes spending the money we are obsessed with saving.

Compatibility goes even deeper. We each have personal flaws. But while my flaws may seem like terrible deal-breakers to some, others may find them merely inconvenient, cute or even endearing. For example, if I had a problem with my temper, it would be less of a problem with someone who was able to tune me out and ignore me than it would with someone overly sensitive, or with an abuse history, or with her own temper problem.

> *Many of our flaws are old*
> *emotional defenses which can*
> *fade away when we're loved*
> *in spite of them.*

I worked with one guy with a temper problem. He would start criticizing his wife, in an unconscious attempt to pick a fight, and she would give him a kiss (and sometimes a tickle.) and tell him to "stop being cranky." It actually worked. He was lucky enough to find someone who could easily handle his temper.

That's compatibility.

Compare that to the couple who would immediately begin yelling, blaming, name-calling, and door-slamming.

Some imperfections are easier for us to ignore than others. Some compatibility issues can work themselves out over time. We can learn to compromise to an extent. We can bargain: "I'll agree to do this for you if you'll agree to do that for me." We can take turns winning: "It's your turn to pick the restaurant/ movie/ TV show/ vacation."

People need to consider compatibility in their relationships. In what areas are we or aren't we compatible? Can it be changed or worked around? Am I ignoring major compatibility issues?

Keeping Romance Alive

"Immature love says: 'I love you because I need you.' Mature love says 'I need you because I love you." ~Erich Fromm

Romantics like me are often curious about how to keep the romance alive in a marriage. If your parents had a healthy, loving marriage, lucky you! Many of us lacked loving role models.

Decades ago, I had a friend named Mel, who taught me a valuable lesson about romantic relationships. Mel had been a high-level executive in a huge corporation. He was a workaholic. He made a ton of money, but his wife took the kids and walked away. She had expected more from marriage.

Mel figured out that his career focus had cost him his family life. He took a lowly clerical position with my company. Something he could walk away from at 5 o'clock. He successfully resisted every one of our attempts to promote him.

Then he met an elementary school teacher. They fell in love and married. They were both from failed marriages and were determined to keep the romance alive in their marriage.

For starters, they didn't own a television. Mel said it forced them to talk with one another, play games and cards, etc. So far as he was concerned, "TV teaches people to sit in the same room and ignore one another." Seemed a bit radical, but I understood what he was saying.

Another thing that impressed me about their relationship was that they got all dressed up and went out every Thursday night. They went to dinner, and then to a movie or a show or dancing depending on what was going on. They had met on a Thursday, so they celebrated their anniversary *every Thursday*.

I once asked Mel if he ever didn't feel like going out some Thursdays. He said, "Sure. I'm sure she feels that way, too, sometimes. But, unless one of us is sick, we get dressed and go and have a good time." They had made a commitment to have a romantic marriage, and they stayed focused on that commitment, rather than what they felt like or didn't feel like from moment to moment.

After more than a decade of marriage, they each wrote each other notes, bought each other little gifts; they did everything they could to make the other feel loved every day.

I spent a lot of time thinking about Mel and his marriage. I learned a lot. I'm not suggesting we all sell our televisions. That was their choice. Nor am I suggesting we celebrate our anniversaries each week. That was their thing, too. What I *am* suggesting is that, if you are a romantic who was lucky enough to find another romantic and you each agree that you want a romantic marriage, you commit to doing whatever it takes to making your partner feel loved, every day. Worry less about what you're *getting* and more about what you're *giving*. If your partner isn't reciprocating, you have a much deeper problem.

A romantic marriage requires the love and commitment of *both* partners. One romantic cannot create a romantic marriage alone. Some couples are roommates with a marriage license, and they like it that way. That's fine. We're not all romantics, nor should we be. But for those who long for the elusive romantic marriage, it does exist. It is possible.

Radical as their approach was, Mel and his wife are still deeply in love. They still look forward to coming home to each other's company each night. They still spend time plotting how to make each other feel loved.

Learning To Be Married

Before Judy and I married, I read an article about which issues most commonly led to marital arguments and failures. One of the most common issues was the division of responsibilities. I could imagine this being a problem for us since Judy had grown up in a family of five women and one man, who all shared household tasks. In contrast, I had grown up in a family of three men and one woman. My mom was responsible for everything domestic. I used to joke that *my* only domestic skill was that I lived in a house.

Though I lived on my own since age 17, I knew little about most domestic tasks, since I was never expected to do any of them. I knew how to cook, pay my bills, and visit the local laundromat when I ran out of clean underwear. My apartment was so messy, one of my best friends joked, "Rick doesn't *live* here – he only comes here to play music and sleep." When I first met Judy, I spent two weeks cleaning my apartment, and it still looked like a four-room dumpster when I finally invited her over.

So, I could imagine us having words over domestic responsibilities.

I got an idea. We first made a list of domestic tasks – grocery shopping, cooking, cleaning, laundry, washing dishes, drying dishes, paying bills, doing taxes, feeding the dog, etc. – Once we had a fairly extensive list we each indicated which tasks we:

1. Enjoyed doing
2. Didn't mind doing
3. Preferred not to do
4. Hated doing

Then we got together and compared lists. We traded and negotiated tasks. It turned out we *both* hated grocery shopping, so we agreed to shop together. We made it fun. We danced in the supermarket aisle until a stranger came around the corner into the aisle. Then I stopped immediately and let Judy get caught.

Okay. Maybe I had *more* fun.

But it worked. We bought in quantity so that we only had to shop for groceries every five or six weeks, the exceptions being when we needed bread or milk and, years later, when our son Mike was born.

From time to time, we revamped our duties, as circumstances changed. Today, Judy works full-time from home while I'm semi-retired. I'm responsible for cooking, laundry, shopping, errands, emptying the dishwasher, researching purchases and services (everything from cars to toasters to lipstick to contractors), etc.

Arguments over finances was another one of the leading causes of marriage failures in the 1980s. When we were dating, I was writing and recording lots of electronic music on synthesizers. I could imagine feeling resentful if Judy began restricting my equipment purchases. I wondered if I would resent her higher-priced personal purchases.

That led to another idea. At the time, I earned twice as much pay as Judy (She would later blow past me when I changed careers.) What if I paid 2/3 of our joint expenses – rent, groceries, gas, etc. – and she was only responsible for 1/3? Whatever was left from each paycheck after expenses would become our personal discretionary money. If either of us got a raise, the percentage we paid toward expenses would increase, and our spouse would also see an increase in their personal share.

It worked. We got excited about each other's personal purchases and never resentful. As the years passed, we expanded the category of joint expenses to include joint savings and vacation funds.

Several times, I shared these strategies with people who thought they sounded "unromantic." My response was, "What's romantic about arguing over money or domestic chores?"

We learned to negotiate. We learned to take turns choosing. All of these strategies allow us more time to enjoy life and each other's company. It allows us more time to make one another feel loved.

THE THERAPY BIZ

Psychotherapeutic Style

"Each person is a unique individual. Hence, psychotherapy should be formulated to meet the uniqueness of the individual's needs, rather than tailoring the person to fit the Procrustean bed of a hypothetical theory of human behavior." ~Milton H. Erickson

Some people assume that all therapists are new-agey hand-holders who just listen and nod like bobbleheads, then **suggest** an astrology reading, a gluten-free diet, and your choice of complimentary love flower or polished healing stone on your way out the door.

That's not me. My job is to help fix what's broken.

I'm friendly and warm and praise my clients for every success on their part, but my style is directive and solution-focused. When my clients make a *poor* choice, I am the mirror that lets them see it was a poor choice.

Some therapists like answering a question with a question: "What do *you* think you should do?" My feeling is, my clients have been doing things *their* way for years and their life isn't working for them. They presumably came to therapy to have someone suggest a *different* way of reacting to a given situation. I would have to be grossly uninterested to ask a client, "What do *you* think you should do?" Nonetheless, some clients respond well to the Socratic method.

I help break the problem down and list the possible choices, along with the advantages and disadvantages of each. Ultimately, my client will decide what to do, but I'll help objectively identify the choices.

One of the most powerful lessons I've learned in this field is that

My ability to help clients is largely dependent on my ability to influence them.

If I don't connect with you powerfully enough to influence you, my treatment will fail. It's why personality compatibility matters.

It's why some new clients think I walk on water while others probably wish I'd drown in it!

Therapy is like any relationship. Not everyone "clicks" with everyone. My office door once had a sign that read, "*If you've got issues, I've got tissues.*" Inside my office, was a sign that read, "*How you do anything, is how you do everything.*"

I believe in truth in advertising.

I'm often asked what a person should look for in a therapist. The asker often expects me to talk about college degrees, licenses and treatment modalities. But I've boiled my answer down to this:

1) Does the therapist seem to sincerely like you?
2) Does the therapist speak in a way that you clearly understand?
3) Does the therapist seem to have a firm, confident grasp of what they can do for you?
4) Did you feel comfortable? Is this someone you might enjoy talking with for an hour a week?

If the answer to any of these is no, that's not your therapist. Don't be afraid to ask for someone else. Most of us don't take it personally. Any therapist who *does* take it personally probably needs therapy worse than *you* do. An emotionally immature or damaged therapist most likely has nothing to teach you anyway.

I remember one colleague who was so obsessive he wasted 25 minutes of an (unpaid, but required) weekly department meeting arguing that the three foot Christmas tree in the waiting room might be offensive to non-Christians. No client had complained. He just went on and on about this while most of us zoned out.

Months later, when this same clinician announced that he was going to start a group therapy session for clients with OCD, I wondered what exactly he imagined he could teach an obsessive person.

People have often asked me what they should look for in a Couples Counselor. My answer consists of one simple question: "Have you ever been in a successful long-term relationship?" It's that simple.

I knew a woman with a license in Marriage and Family Counseling who was in her late 20s and on her fourth husband! What could she possibly teach anyone about maintaining or rescuing a relationship?

~:~:~:~:~

Another difference among therapists is the relative skill in conducting a diagnostic interview. I once was assigned a 45-year-old female client whose chart indicated a previous failed suicide attempt. Needing more details, I asked her about it:

Q. "How long ago was this suicide attempt?"

A. "I was 15 at the time."

Q. "And what exactly did you do?"

A. "I tried to overdose."

Q. "On what?"

A. "Aspirin."

Q. "How many aspirins did you take?"

A. "Maybe four or five."

Q. "Did you think that would kill you?"

A. "Of course not! My boyfriend at the time was being a jerk. I wanted to scare him."

Our intake clinician would have had a "failed suicide attempt" on this woman's medical record for life. Imagine that coming up at a child custody hearing one day? Often, inexperienced clinicians are uncomfortable asking detailed questions.

I was no different. When I began treating people in my first mental health agency, I felt awkward asking women personal questions about sex. Knowing that it was important didn't make it easier.

I had one client who complained about her husband "the asshole" every session. All she ever talked about was the insensitive things he did and said and how terribly he treated her. After listening to this for weeks, I was convinced that this guy was an asshole, and this marriage had no future.

One day, I realized I didn't have the whole picture yet. I suppose I could guess the answer, but I needed to ask:

Q. "When was the last time you and your husband had sex?"

A. "This morning."

(?!)

Q. "How often do you have sex?"

A. "Every day, once or twice a day."

(If I were a dog, my ears would have folded back.)

Q. "And you've been married for ten years?"

A. "Yeah. To the same asshole."

Sometimes you just don't have enough information unless you ask the right questions. Eventually, I was able to ask complete strangers about sex, menstrual cycles, masturbation, fetishes, and such as though they were normal conversation.

I do try to restrict those questions to the office, though.

One client described her hysterectomy as, "The best thing I ever did! It turned a factory into a playground."

Another factor that plays a large part in a clinician's therapeutic style is the ability to focus on the client's complaint. Some clinicians bring their personal baggage to the table. They meet clients, get a handle on their personality and lifestyle choices, and then proceeds to fix what *they* think is wrong, despite the client's original complaint.

A good illustration of this was Desiree Moore. Desiree came into my office wearing a dress so tight, you could see her freckles. In the course of her intake session, Desiree revealed that the source of her income was posting nude photos of herself online. "Customers" who bought a "membership" to her website had the privilege of seeing her nude photos taken by her husband.

To be brutally honest, to say that Desiree was an attractive woman would be a bold-faced lie. I wasn't the least bit curious about what was going on beneath that sprayed-on dress. But she told me stories of how, when her car died, several customers offered to give her a car. No charge. Now and then, a customer expressed a desire and a willingness to pay to "meet" Desiree and get a motel room. Desiree was willing to do this, but she insisted on her husband being present when she met the guy initially. Only if hubby gave the thumbs up, did the couple go off and get a motel room. "I'm not a *hooker* or anything!"

Here's the thing: Desiree did not seek me out to fix her lifestyle. Her lifestyle worked perfectly well for her. She had begun having panic attacks and wanted them to stop. That was our work to-gether. Any opinion or judgment I might have had about Desiree, her marriage, or her profession, was irrelevant. My job was simply to teach her to turn off her panic attacks.

That's not how some clinicians work. You come in complaining about panic attacks, which they might have no idea how to treat, or they discount as irrelevant. They decide what's *really* wrong with you and proceed to treat *that*. Of course, since they're treating a part of you that doesn't give you any trouble you're aware of, you're unmotivated to change, and treatment fails.

If you brought your car to a mechanic and asked for new brake pads, you'd be horrified if he rebuilt your engine, painted your car a different color, and handed you a bill for thousands of dollars.

I see myself as an "emotional mechanic." It's not my place to give you a paint job or an engine overhaul just because I think you could use one. Why would you spend any time, money, or effort unless you perceive a problem? If you come to me complaining of panic attacks or your fear of dogs, that's what we're going to work on because that's your complaint. If I'm successful, you may just mention another troublesome part of your personality. You may ask whether anything can be done about it. Maybe, some years from now, you'll want my help with a marital problem.

I've seen clinicians go as far as to assume someone has been a victim of sexual trauma when the client has no such recollection. The argument is "They've blocked it from their memory." If that's true (very rare), then it's because the person isn't ready or equipped to handle the memory. If that's the case, it's reckless to treat it.

When I studied hypnotherapy with Dr. Brown, he said that there had been more than 4000 cases in the U.S. court system where clients had recalled trauma under hypnosis *after* it was suggested by the hypnotherapist. If I were to ask you, under hypnosis, how old you were when the hippopotamus sat on your ice cream cone, you would report an age at random. If I asked you, "Who touched your genitals when you were in fourth grade?" you'd name a random person.

Scary, huh?

It's the main reason that information gleaned under hypnosis is inadmissible in court.

No one comes into therapy asking to be self-actualized. They come with specific problems. We need to help them fix those problems or refer them to someone who can. One reason that Dr. John Twomey was my favorite professor in grad school was his conviction that we, as therapists, should position ourselves on the same level as our patients and clients. He insisted we be human with them, that we allow something of ourselves to come through. That's difficult for some clinicians. Some feel safer hiding behind an emotional wall. How likely am I to influence you from behind an emotional wall?

One of my gay male clients was upset because the pastor of his Christian church had arrogantly announced that gay people were an abomination and would never be allowed into Heaven. This had deeply disturbed my client. It hurt me that a religious leader would be so callously hateful and hurtful. I told my client, "Different people have different ideas of 'Heaven.' Each person's vision of 'Heaven' is a mirror of that particular person." By now, I was getting tears in my eyes because of what I was about to say:

"There will be gay people in *my* Heaven."

We both sat there in tears, looking at each other. There was nothing I did or said in the entire time I worked with him that made the impact that moment did.

The truth is, I don't even believe in heaven. But I believe even less in hating and hurting people from behind a pulpit. I felt that my best chance of countering the damage his pastor had done was to open up my heart.

Sometimes psychotherapy is listening, mirroring, teaching tricks and techniques, and suggesting alternative behaviors. But sometimes it's being real and present and human in the presence of another human being.

Of course, trying to help some people is like trying to pick up a turd by the clean side.

There are clients who don't get better. There are clients who get huge secondary gains from doing exactly what they're doing. Others are just too afraid to try doing anything differently. ("the devil you know.")

The way I see it, my clients' successes or failures are theirs, not mine. I'm just the tour guide. Mine is the easy part. When I have clients who aren't making progress, and I know I've tried every trick I know, I gently suggest they may not be ready to do this yet, or perhaps another clinician would have better luck. I prepare to cut them loose. Some of them get serious and start doing the work. Some are relieved that I'm cutting them loose. Some return for treatment when their lives become even less manageable.

A therapist who can't let go is a therapist who can't teach anyone else to let go.

Someone once told me, "With the possible exception of Substance Abuse, never treat a condition that you have or are recovering from."

I believe that's often true. I have the ability to be objective with trauma survivors and clients with anxiety issues. I can be objective with schizophrenics. I am less objective with depression.

I've known competent clinicians who were survivors of domestic abuse who did a miserable job of dealing with couples issues because they had lost the ability to be objective about relationships. I'm not suggesting that there are no exceptions, but it is a common mistake.

We can't be experts on everything. When I intake a client with an eating disorder or an attention disorder, I let them know up front that I will be transferring them to a clinician specifically trained to work with that disorder.

I had a colleague who was a dear friend. She had been seeing a client for panic attacks for three years. She didn't know how to treat panic attacks and spent three years talking to the client about the client's childhood. When the client finally expressed her wish to stop therapy, since her panic attacks were no less frequent after all this time, our clinical manager suggested the client work with me. Two months later, we terminated treatment. No more panic attacks.

I've known lots of clinicians who treat conditions for which they don't specifically know any treatments. They wind up digging around the client's childhood or life choices, hoping to find something they can work with. Once again, the key is knowing when to let go.

When someone comes in for an oil change, we should change their damn oil or send them to someone who can. Therapists shouldn't paint the car instead and then expect clients to pay.

Psychotherapeutic Methods

"The important thing about theories isn't whether they're right or wrong. It's whether or not they're useful."
~Sandra Rasmussen, Ph.D.

The therapeutic method involves choices. I don't expect every professional to agree with me, but I believe that it is our responsibility, as therapists, to have more than one tool in our box.

In grad school, when our Counseling Techniques professor said that Rogerian Therapy or "Client-Centered Therapy" was the easiest to learn he made converts out of half the class.

Rogerian Therapy is described as "active listening with unconditional positive regard". The therapist sits at the edge of his chair, leaning toward the client so that his body language conveys the message, "I find you absolutely fascinating!" The dialog can sound like this:

Client: "My husband can be so infuriating sometimes."

Therapist: "So, what I hear you saying is that your husband sometimes causes you to feel frustrated and angry."

Client: "Yes. That would be a definition of the word, 'infuriating'."

or

Client: "Sometimes I feel like I can't get out of my own way."

Therapist: "What I hear you saying is that sometimes you feel like your actions are ineffective in helping you achieve your goals. How does *that* make you feel?"

Client: "Ummm... Like I can't get out of my own way?"

(I'm parodying intentionally here.)

Rogerian Therapy always struck me as superficial and artificial. You can practice it without paying much attention to what is going on with your client. You listen to the words, and you spit words back.

I once heard the argument that Rogerian Therapy was the only therapy in which you could "do no harm." I completely disagree with this. The Rogerian therapist but lets the client lead. The fact is, clients don't always go to healthy places, and delving deeply into unhealthy places is seldom a good strategy. Rogerian Therapy has some value in establishing trust. (How can you dislike someone who finds you absolutely fascinating?) It's a viable choice for clinicians conducting client intakes, but most people and illnesses respond better to other treatment approaches.

Another therapy for which I have limited respect is psychoanalysis or "psychodynamic therapy" as it is often called today. Freud was the Henry Ford of psychology. He was the pioneer. He discovered things that remain relevant today (transference, repression, the unconscious, projection, etc.), but many of his theories, especially those concerning infantile sexual trauma being at the root of most mental illness and the Oedipus Complex and Penis Envy stuff is less useful. Worst was his belief that once you understood the basis and origin of your neurosis, it would magically disappear. Also, as Fritz Perls said, "To mature means to take responsibility for your life. Psychoanalysis fosters the infantile state by considering that the past is responsible for the illness."

My favorite clinical supervisor, Michael Meleedy, and I should have never got along. He was trained in psychodynamic therapy, and I was a fan of nearly every *other* type of therapy. But Michael respected my ability to creatively develop techniques to fit my clients, and I was in awe of his ability to get me "unstuck".

Several times, I reached a point with clients where they became unmotivated or somehow stuck, and I was unable to get them moving forward. I would explain the situation to Michael during my supervision hour, and he would always suggest something simple and brilliant without even thinking hard about it. Had we not moved from Massachusetts, I would have happily worked with Michael until one of us retired.

Before I discuss what I consider some viable and useful therapies, I'll throw out this idea:

Three things make up who we are as individuals: what we think, what we feel, and what we do. If we manage to change any one of these three aspects of ourselves, the other two will follow.

Cognitive Therapy* is a must for any therapist's bag of tricks. Cognitive therapy works to change your *thinking*. Clients are taught to argue a healthy position internally.

For example:

Client's automatic thought: "I'm a useless piece of shit."

Client's new argumentative thought: "No I'm not! I'm a good husband. I try hard to be a good dad. I'm pretty good at my job. I have friends who like me and care about me."

Client's revised thought: "Okay. Maybe I'm not *useless*."

Cognitive techniques can be very helpful. An added benefit is that the client is now in a position to self-correct outside the therapy session. Cognitive therapy* is considered the most effective treatment for depression. It is also a very effective treatment for low self-esteem. Rational-Emotive Therapy falls into this category.

* *I seldom use the popular and accepted term, "Cognitive-Behavioral Therapy," because it rarely contains a behavioral component.*

Gestalt Therapy, Psychodrama, Primal Scream Therapy, etc. work by directly affecting a client's *feelings*. When I was in my late teens, I was sure I wanted to be a Gestalt Therapist. I even saw a gestalt therapist in Boston just to experience the treatment.

My most vivid memory of this was the session when the therapist worked on my repressed anger. He had me shouting and yelling until I connected with my anger.

Then I got on the bus and went home. That night I was leaving the living room to head to the kitchen. My mother had a decorative wooden birdcage hanging against a wall. The wooden corner of the birdcage stabbed my shoulder as I walked past it. Without even a thought, my arm came up and pulverized that poor birdcage. I turned that stupid wooden birdcage into splinters! This wasn't the first time it poked me, but it would be the *last time*. Fortunately, my mother blamed her poor choice of placement, rather than my having unlocked my anger. A day or two later, while barefooted, I stubbed my toe on the leg of the kitchen table and retaliated by kicking it hard as I could. Not one of my brightest moments. Today, I can turn my anger on or off at will, depending on the situation. I had to *find* it before I could learn to express and control it.

The downside to Gestalt therapy is that it is more brutal than many clients are willing to endure. Its founder, Dr. Fritz Perls, used to claim that he could free anyone from neurosis in ten sessions or less, and I don't doubt that he could, but the client would be in for some very intense and uncomfortable sessions. In fact, many of the therapies that directly target people's *feelings* make people very uncomfortable.

Targeting what a person *does* sums up the behavioral approach. Behavioral techniques are vital. Examples are Acceptance and Commitment Therapy (ACT), Reality Therapy, Operant Conditioning, Exposure techniques, etc.

Behavioral therapies have the best track record with anxiety disorders, but they can also be very effective with clients who don't respond well to cognitive techniques.

I once treated an executive who couldn't get back on a plane after a traumatic flight from China. The guy was a buyer for a major U.S. retailer. International flights were a part of his job. I had three weeks to get him on a plane without drugs.

He committed to seeing me twice a week and doing homework each night. I took him through a progressive desensitization exercise during our sessions and had him do them on his own each evening.

Progressive desensitization, in this case, involved his imagining each step of the flight process from packing his luggage at home to take off and ascent. We broke this down into dozens of steps. He imagined each step in the safety of my office. When the anxiety became too much for him, we returned to step one and started over again.

Three weeks later, he boarded a plane without drugs. His company would never know there was ever a problem. That's a good example of an effective behavioral technique.

One therapy technique that defies categorization is the story-telling technique. We all have defenses and sometimes don't want to hear direct advice. As a therapist, I may know exactly what you *need* to know but, unless you figure it out for *yourself*, you may not learn it. In some cases, my best approach will be to quietly and subtly plant a seed in your mind and hope that it will grow on its own. The best way to do that is by telling a story.

Dave Disaster was a heroin addict/dealer with a mood disorder. He was in and out of jail constantly. During the time I worked with him, he was sentenced to prison twice. Once for six months and once for a year. Dave was one of those white guys in his 20s who spoke, acted, and dressed like an inner city black gang member. He took great delight in telling me about the 23 times he cheated on his girlfriend, who was the mother of his child. He was outraged and ended the relationship the one time when she cheated on *him*.

He once did a drug deal on his cell phone from my office! I made him shut off his phone at the start of each session after that.

Dave's life was a real mess.

I remembered that, when we first met, he mentioned that he had written some rap music lyrics some years ago. So, I casually mentioned my alcoholic friend who had just got hired as a bass player in a working band. Dave was interested, so I gave him some details and then suggested we get back to our session.

I had no such friend. The story was total bullshit. I was hoping to plant a seed.

Weeks later, Dave asked what vocal microphones I preferred, since he knew that I was also a musician. A few weeks after that, he showed up for his session with a brown paper bag. In it was a Shure SM58 vocal mike. Dave started doing some rap singing at a few local clubs and planned to do some recording as well.

At this point, I'd love to end the story by telling you that Dave recently won a Grammy Award but, in fact, when we moved from Maine, Dave was back in prison.

Nonetheless, storytelling can be a powerful seed-planting tool. Sometimes I tell true stories, and sometimes I make them up. The important thing is to plant that seed while the client's defenses are down so that the client can arrive at a solution on his own.

If any of my former clients read this and recall me telling stories, I apologize.

I did say that I was sneaky.

Dual Relationships with Clients

Dual relationships with clients are relationships outside the office simultaneous with treatment. It means going to the movies or a party with a client, buying from or selling to a client, entering into a romantic relationship with a client.

This issue first came up for me in grad school.

In Massachusetts, at the time, psychotherapists were required to wait two years after the therapy was over before they could establish a "dual relationship" (friendship, love affair, etc.) with a client. Marriage Counselors were only required to wait six months. A woman in my class disagreed with that license provision because, "What if you happen to fall in love with a client?"

I argued that we don't fall in love helplessly and unavoidably like in a Harlequin Romance novel. We make an adult choice to fall in love. Can you imagine how often we would fall in love with children, relatives, or our friends' spouses if adults fell helplessly in love without any sense of judgment?

We *allow* ourselves to fall in love, or we don't. Sadly, there are therapists who allow themselves to fall in love with clients.

Clients and patients often become infatuated with their therapists because the therapist is often one of the few people who listens to and sincerely cares about them. The client can speak freely with the therapist without jeopardizing the relationship. This feels very much like love, to some clients, and can generate feelings of affection toward the therapist.

Confronting this directly can be humiliating for the client unless done very carefully. I will sometimes share a story using my marriage as an example to teach a lesson about appropriate relationships. Hidden underneath the surface is the clear message that I am happily married and in love with my wife. Most women got the message without being humiliated.

Emotionally-grounded therapists don't take infatuation personally. I bear in mind that the same client would fall for *any* caring male therapist who occupied my chair. As a therapist, I have to be aware of the boundary between myself and a female client. I'm here for her; she is not here for me. While I know her better than most, she only knows my work persona. It is not a balanced relationship nor will it ever be. The therapist has too much power to manipulate the client and the relationship.

It is unusual for a male therapist to see as many sexual trauma survivors as I do. My female clients perceive me as "safe" and easy to talk with. I'm not "checking them out." I don't flirt, and I never suggest that our relationship is anything but therapeutic. Most of them know that I'm happily married. Many sexual trauma clients feel that it's quite powerful when a person of the same sex that caused the pain has helped them heal that pain.

Sometimes a client will ask for a hug. I give great hugs, but it's important that my client understands that my hugs are not sexual or romantic in any way. I'll never initiate a hug. Clients have to ask.

I estimate that I've seen more than 2000 patients and clients in my career. Of that number, I have come away with four friends: two men and two women.

In each case, they are friendships like any other. We don't discuss psychotherapy. They don't come to me with mental health problems. We talk about the same sort of things that any friends would.

Psychotherapeutic Reality

Let's be honest. Not all clients succeed. Some clients shrug off everything that's suggested and say it doesn't work. They're right. It doesn't, because they're not even considering doing it.

Some clients didn't come for help. They only wanted to complain once a week and have someone listen to them. Some are coerced into therapy by a loved one, then go home and complain how awful the therapist was.

Some clients are getting secondary gains from their complaints. The guy with depression whose wife treats him with kid gloves and whose children tiptoe around him won't admit it but, deep down, it makes him feel special, and he's not sure he wants to give that up. Every mental illness has the potential for secondary gains.

Some people quit therapy because they hate feeling put "on the spot," hate talking about themselves or looking within. A lot of men fall into this category. I used to quip that women come for therapy at the first sign of trouble, whereas we meet men after their first suicide attempt. Fortunately, that has become less true over the years.

Some clients are motivated in session but lose motivation as soon as they walk out the door and step back into their lives. I've had clients ask me if they'd still be eligible for disability if we make the illness go away. Some clients we never hear from again after their initial intake. Not all clients succeed.

I've been asked if I could tell who would succeed in therapy and who wouldn't. The fact is, some people show up complaining that their life sucks, and it's all because of their spouse, kids, in-laws, co-workers, boss, or neighbors. Those people fail because they place the blame elsewhere. They take no responsibility for their part. Change is not an option. Others come in complaining that their life sucks, and they think that *they* might be doing something wrong. Those people succeed.

Everyone reacts to us. I can't change everyone one person at a time, but if I change *myself*, those around me will change, because they will react to the new me. The only way I can change my life is to change me.

Clients can surprise you. Barroom Bob showed up drunk for his 11:00 AM intake. My office was on the second floor, and I purposely walked up the stairs behind him in case he fell. He climbed the stairs with both hands on the banister. Bob was 44 years old, but he looked like he could be 70.

Once inside my office, it soon became apparent that he was too drunk to answer many of the intake questions. I put down the intake forms and said, "I'm going to stop the intake here. The best advice I can give you is to admit yourself to a detox facility." Bob muttered, "I ain't going to no detox! They don't let you drink!"

I gave him some phone numbers and local addresses and said, "If you should ever do a 30-day detox and you still want to work with me, I'll be happy to work with you. Did you drive here?"

It turned out he walked. He lived about five blocks away. The sidewalks were icy, so I gave him a ride home. (This is not done by most agency clinicians, but we did this all the time at the Vet Center, and I just wanted him to get home safely.)

I would have bet a week's pay that I would never see this guy again. C'mon, he's drunk at 11:00 AM and "They don't let you drink in detox!" I half-expected him to be dead before he turned 50.

Five or six weeks later I got a call from a woman who said she was Bob's girlfriend. "Bob is getting out of detox on Monday, and he said that you were willing to work with him." At first, I wasn't even sure who she was talking about. When I realized who Bob was, I set up an appointment.

We worked well together. Bob suffered one relapse but, otherwise, stayed sober. His goal was to go back to school and learn computers. The Massachusetts Rehabilitation Commission had a program that offered occupational training. That was Bob's dream.

Mass. Rehab told Bob that, if he stayed sober for six months, they would consider him for a training program. As soon as he had six months sobriety to his credit, he contacted them again.

They told him they would consider him in *another* six months.

He was crushed. He was so proud of himself and ready to learn computers. They didn't even want to meet with him. Six months later, Bob proudly walked in their office, and was told, "Six months more."

Bob became depressed. He kept showing up for his appointments, but now he was talking about killing himself. He had no real plan in place, but he was that depressed.

One day, he practically danced his way into my office.

Rick: "Hi Bob! What's going on?"

Bob: "Last week I was walking along Main Street and guess what I saw?"

Rick: "What?"

Bob: "The library! Did you ever think that you can walk into a library and learn anything you want to learn? I started with the beginners computer books. Fuck Mass. Rehab. I'm learning computers! They even have computers there that anyone can use."

(When I relocated from Massachusetts to Maine, Bob was still sober. The day we met, I would have bet a week's pay that I would never see Barroom Bob again. I would have lost.)

Sometimes clients have given me way more credit than was due. I saw a woman who couldn't lift her right arm as high as shoulder level. After months of doctor visits and hospital tests, it was determined that the cause was psychological, and she was referred to me. We met weekly, and she talked about her past and present stressors. After about four or five weeks of this, she came to my office one morning and showed me how she could effortlessly lift her arm straight over her head. I congratulated her, and we terminated treatment.

Two years later, I got a call from her. "Remember me? You fixed my arm a few years ago. Well, I can't lift my arm again. I need you to say whatever it was you said two years ago that made my arm work."

<sigh>

"I can't do therapy by phone, but let's set up an appointment."

There are times when people have surprised me by coming up with their own coping strategies.

One woman who I was treating for relationship issues mentioned that she used to have severe panic attacks. I asked how they stopped. She said that she would go to the bathroom, strip off all of her clothes, and lie down on the cold tile floor. That stopped her panic attacks immediately. She would even do this while visiting other people's homes. When she felt a panic attack coming on, she excused herself, did her thing, and people just assumed she was using the toilet. The panic attacks eventually stopped coming.

Another client had a serious case of PTSD due to sexual trauma. The first time she came to see me one of our support staff came into my office to tell me confidentially that my next client looks like she "needs real help."

"She's wearing a pair of antenna on her head!" she warned.

According to my notes, this client wanted help with a marital issue. She hadn't been released from a mental hospital or anything. I was intrigued. I went to the waiting room and, sure enough, a woman was sitting there with two antennae with little red balls on the ends bobbing about over her head, reading a magazine.

"Princess Zia from the planet Zoltar?"

Zia smiled appropriately and followed me into my office. "What's with the antenna?" I asked.

"I have PTSD, and I'm not very comfortable making small talk with strangers. I learned a long time ago that if I do something goofy like this, people keep their distance," she replied.

As I got to know Zia, I learned that she had come up with all sorts of interesting and creative ways of managing her PTSD symptoms. She only needed me to help her with some marital intimacy issues.

I would never tell a PTSD sufferer to wear antennae in public. Nor would I tell someone with panic disorder to strip off their clothes and lie on a cold tile floor in someone's bathroom, but when a client finds a way of coping that works, I don't mess with it.

My best memory of Zia was one Halloween when she sat in our waiting room dressed as a witch. Not just a witch costume, mind you. It was so detailed; she looked like she walked off a Hollywood horror movie set!

That Halloween, I came to get my clients from the waiting room wearing a glow-in-the-dark hockey goalie's mask on my face, and a sign hung around my neck that read:

"Psycho -Therapist"

Every one of my clients knew it was me.

QUESTIONS AND ANSWERS

I'm asked questions daily on various psychology online forums, often touching on subjects that don't warrant entire chapters. I've included some here. When I get vague or silly questions, I'm not above giving silly answers.

Q. My wife is full of bad habits and is extremely resistant to change. For example, she never turns off the lights when she leaves a room. What should I do?

A. I can answer this one quite easily using a personal example:

I suppose my mother must have drilled into my head the rule that you always put things back in the refrigerator after you use them. No matter what I use, butter, mayonnaise, *anything*, I promptly put it back in the fridge when I'm done.

Then I got married. And my wife, who I love dearly, would take out a bottle of salad dressing, drizzle some on her salad, and walk away, leaving the bottle out on the counter. It drove me nuts! I would tell her, "You left the salad dressing on the counter." and she would reply, "Oh! Could you put it away, please?"

What?? I didn't take it out! Why should I put it away? These were my thoughts as my resentment grew. Finally, I decided it was time to confront the issue head-on.

"You know I don't appreciate having to put things back in the fridge when you forget to put them away." which, of course, would lead to an argument.

I wasn't a therapist yet. I was just a new husband learning to live with a wife.

One day, after one of these arguments (which I hated) I looked at whatever it was she had left on the counter and a thought came to me: We just had a huge argument over 50 cents worth of product at the bottom of a jar. Putting that stupid jar back in the fridge is obviously more important to *me* than it is to *her*. Is this worth an argument? If this is so important to me, why don't I just put the jar back in the fridge (so that I feel better) and skip the argument (so that I feel better)?

By this time, I *was* a therapist.

How many times did my wife pick up after me without treating it like a big deal warranting a discussion, an argument or a major behavioral change?

So, my answer to you (in case it isn't obvious) is turn off the light if it bothers you. And do it *because* it bothers you. Whatever other "bad habits" she has: the same answer. Presumably, you married her because you love her. Presumably, she married you in spite of *your* flaws.

Don't play teacher or behavioral coach. *Quietly* take care of the stuff that bugs you and enjoy your wife and your marriage.

After 32 years of marriage, I still quietly pick up after my wife and she still quietly picks up after me. We talk about things

that interest us and spend our time doing *fun* things together. We rarely argue, and we are still very much in love with one another.

Q. What secret side to human nature do therapists see that would surprise non-therapists?

A. I'll give you my favorite one: *People create precisely what they try hardest to avoid.*

Germaphobes and obsessive types put paper on public toilet seats and let it fall on the floor when they're finished because they don't dare touch it. They don't flush because they don't dare touch the flush handle. So, when you walk into a public restroom with toilet paper all over the floor and a toilet full of wretched feces, you blame the low-class slobs or chalk it up to vandalism, but it's the neat freaks that made the mess!

People who are afraid of being treated unfairly will unintentionally treat others unfairly in an attempt to ensure that no one is taking advantage of them.

It's a fascinating phenomenon which I have seen in hundreds of people time and again.

(Before the townspeople start coming up my driveway with pitchforks and torches, I should point out that not all neat freaks leave public restrooms a mess. Many have learned to knock their toilet seat paper into the bowl and flush the toilet with their shoe, the leading cause of flush-handle breakage in the US. They have elevated public peeing and pooping to an art form.)

Q. My wife of 24 years is 53. I am 47, and I am in love with a 24-year-old. My wife is dependent on me. This girl is saying that if I want any more sex, I must separate from my wife now. What should I do?

A. I had a friend who was married for 20+ years. Both he and his wife were awesome, happily-married people. Then the 45-year-old guy fell in love with a 23-year-old married woman. They both got divorced and married one another. When his 2nd wife turned 45, she left my friend for a 30-something-year-old guy.

My friend died alone.

We get what we give.

Leaving your wife for the 24-year-old inadvertently gives the 24-year-old permission to do the same when she gets bored with you or enchanted by someone new. Your kids will learn the same lesson.

The 24-year-old is using *sex* to manipulate and blackmail you now. If it *works*, it will work in the future. Sex won't be about expressing love. It'll be your prize for doing whatever she wants — not exactly the basis of a mature, loving relationship.

You had a mid-life crisis and slept with a 24-year-old. Good for you. Now go home and keep your promise.

Q. I told my boyfriend I'm not comfortable being sexually intimate at this stage of the relationship, and he told me I was being selfish, demanding, and unfair to him, because as a guy he has his needs. Am I really?

A. A guy who is in love with you will be patient until you're ready. A guy who is just looking for sex will try to manipulate you into it.

...which is what your boyfriend is trying to do.

Q. What are your thoughts on spouses taking their partners for granted?

A. Let's use a toaster as an analogy. When we want to make toast, we go to our toaster, drop in some bread, push down the handle, wait a bit, and out comes the toast. Simple. Reliable.

When we don't want toast, we don't think about our toaster. We can go days or weeks without thinking about our toaster. It requires no maintenance or attention of any kind. It doesn't take up much space, so it doesn't even get in our way. It's there when we need toast and invisible when we don't.

Some of my clients' partners think they're married to toasters. They expect them to be there to perform whatever service is needed: sex, chores, driver, escort, cook, personal shopper, accountant, mechanic, confidant, adviser, whatever, but expect them to be invisible when that job is done.

They should require no maintenance and no attention. They should have no needs requiring reciprocal services of any kind. It's silly to imagine your toaster needing something from you. We just use our toasters until they can't make toast anymore.

Then we blame the toaster because it didn't last forever.

Q. My girlfriend always makes mistakes. I get very angry, she gets mad, and we always fight. Do I have the right to be angry?

A. Anyone has the right to be angry. It's a normal human emotion. BUT, unlike our other emotions, we can express anger poorly. Part of becoming mature *emotionally* is knowing when and how to express anger. If your girlfriend's "mistakes" and your anger always lead to fights, you're doing it wrong.

Your anger does *not* give you permission to do or say just anything that comes to mind. Your anger is not an excuse to treat your girlfriend less than lovingly.

You're not saying what her "mistakes" are, but you're clear that they're mistakes. If they're truly mistakes and you *know* they're mistakes, why the anger? Surely *you* make mistakes. Don't the people who love you forgive *your* mistakes? People who care about us don't get *angry* at our mistakes.

Q. How can I approach the weight problem that my girlfriend has? I'm feeling less attracted to her as before.

A. Cut her loose so that she can find someone who loves her for *herself.*

Q. Does God recognize gay marriage?

A. That would depend on your personal perception of God. If you believe that God is small-minded, hateful and intolerant as the *worst* of us, then I suppose you would imagine your God to be hateful and against *lots* of things, including gay marriage. If, on the other hand, you believe God to be fairer and more loving than the *best* of us, you would imagine a loving, fair and inclusive God.

How we each imagine God says more about *us* than it does about gods.

Q. How do I find a sex partner?

A. Feel around under the sheets. When you find a leg that isn't yours, you've found your sex partner! It works every time.

Q. What does it mean when a person will try to make someone happy just to get someone to like them and to be with them?

A. I think the key to this question is "just to get someone to like them."

It implies that the person isn't doing this to be kind or loving but to manipulate for their own self-interest.

I've worked with lots of "people-pleasers" and co-dependents. Here is what is unavoidable: if I fool you into loving me by creating a false persona, I'll never know whether you would even *like* the real me; I'll have to keep up that act to keep your love, and I'll always know that you're in love with the "act" and not me.

Q. How do you know if your boyfriend doesn't love you anymore?

A. When you feel someone else's feet in bed, and they're not his.

Q. My husband always drags me to things I hate. Horror movies, wrestling matches, stock car races. But he never wants to come with me to visit my family when I want to.

A. My wife and I give each other space. I'm not obligated to attend Shakespeare events, and she is not obligated to attend my band rehearsals. It works the same with family visits. If either of us wants to visit relatives, the other is not obligated to suffer through it.

But, we have an agreement: Each of us has the option to say, "It's important to me that you accompany me this time." We don't overuse it. I would estimate that each of us invokes that option no more than three times per year.

When this happens, the other goes along, no complaints, no arguments, no sulking. You go because this one time is important to your partner. It's easy to do when you bear in mind all those times you weren't required to go, and you have the same option when her attendance is important to you.

It's a healthy way of handling events and family obligations. My wife and I, who are essentially opposites, have been together successfully for 36 years.

Q. I'm 20 years old. I've had two serious relationships, neither of which worked out. Should I be worried?

A. When you and I learned to walk, we took a step and fell on our bum. Then we got up and took a few steps – and fell on our bum again. (This is why babies are built so low to the ground.)

The only reason that you and I can walk today is because we fell on our bum enough times. We learn relationship skills the same way, by falling on our figurative bums. In fact, we learn *most* life skills that way!

Be patient with yourself. Figure out what you learned from each relationship.

Here is one more fact to bear in mind:

> *We make every important life decision based on inadequate information.*

We hope that our new relationship, home, car, job, or marriage will work out, but it doesn't always. And there is often no way you could have known in advance.

I didn't meet my wife until I was 26. Uncommon people take longer to find love because they need uncommon partners. At least, that's what I tell myself.

Q. Why is emotional abuse harder to recover from than physical abuse?

A. Because most physical pain heals.

Emotional pain is tougher. It stays with us, becomes a part of our psyche and our self-image. Emotional abuse becomes a voice that plays in our head, reminding us that we are flawed and undeserving. If I repeatedly tell a child or a spouse that she's stupid, she will hear those words each time she makes a mistake or fails at something, even long after I'm gone.

Q. Have you ever successfully treated a gambling addiction?

A. Only once. I got a client to commit to tearing two one-dollar bills into tiny pieces and throwing them away each time he gambled. It didn't matter if he gambled at the casino in Connecticut or simply bought a lottery ticket. He agreed to tear up the two dollars, and he did it. His gambling became less frequent and eventually stopped. (I can't say for how long.)

This doesn't work for most people because, even if they agree to do it, they feel like the gambling loss is enough and skip the two dollar ritual, but it can be a powerful negative reinforcer for some who commit to doing it. For those, it can help in curbing many negative behaviors because it sucks to tear up money. Trust me; I've done this myself.

Q. When people in their 60s and older look back on their lives, what common regrets do they have?

A. Their age.

Q. How can I tell if someone is emotionally abusive?

A. Someone who is truly in love with you will consistently try to make you feel *good* about yourself.

Someone who is emotionally abusive will consistently make you feel *worse* about yourself.

Q. You say we avoid what we fear. Isn't it true that we *should* avoid some of the things we fear?

A. There are two types of fears: real and imagined. It is healthy to fear heights or crossing a busy intersection in New Your City. Fears such as these make us hypervigilant, boost our adrenaline, and increase our chance of survival. On the other hand, the fear of kittens or butterflies serves no practical purpose. Many fears save us from no actual threats.

As a result, while avoiding real threats to our safety is wise, people with anxiety disorders tend to limit their life choices or cripple themselves into immobility based on their *imagined* fears.

To use germaphobia (mysophobia) as an example, to wash my hands before dinner or cover my mouth when I cough in public or avoid shaking hands with someone who has a cold are easy and wise practices. But the person who stands at an elevator door for 20 minutes waiting for someone else to push the button because they don't have a tissue to protect them from imagined germs has a mental illness. Their belief that they can insulate themselves from germs is ridiculous. Their fear limits their normal functioning, and that is the key. Any fear that limits your normal, healthy functioning crosses the line into mental illness.

Q. How does a female with a phobia of blood deal with her period?

A. By making lots of yucky faces five days per month.

Q. How can I stop worrying about what others think of me?

A. I have a theory that has served me well: 10% of all the people you'll meet will like you, no matter what. Another 10% will hate you, no matter what. The other 80% has no feelings about you either way. They don't know you exist and don't care.

You don't believe me? Think about the last ten people you encountered, whether they were cashiers, waiters, or just shared a waiting room with you. How many of the last ten can you remember? How many made an impact?

10% is PLENTY.

Those 10% are your "peeps", your tribe. You can be yourself with them. They are attracted to you exactly the way you are. They are people whose souls just resonate with yours. Who knows why? They don't ask you to prove anything. They like you despite your differing opinions. They like you despite your bad choices. They like you despite your failures. They are happy for your every success, in contrast to that 10% who can't stand you, who dislike you even more with each success.

We'll never win over that 90%. Why waste the energy? Why try to change yourself to please them? Better to deal with them with a polite detachment and spend your emotional energy on your 10%.

10% is PLENTY!

One more piece of advice: Go through your address book. Circle the names of the people who energize, enlighten, entertain or inspire you and cross out the names of those who drain your energy.

"If you need encouragement, praise, pats on the back from everybody, then you make everybody your judge." ~Fritz Perls

Q. What constitutes good mental health?
A. Legend has it that Freud once answered this very question. I seldom quote Freud, but I love this answer. He said, *"Mental health is the ability to love, work, and play."*

Let's reverse this. People with mental illnesses often have trouble with one or more of the following:

1) Forming and maintaining healthy relationships

2) Doing meaningful, productive, and satisfying work.

3) Relaxing, being playful with others, or having a healthy sense of humor.

Q. How do I overcome stage fright?
A. I grew up with a fear of public speaking.

Since then I've been on TV and radio lots of times. I've both performed and given talks in front of huge audiences. How do you do that *without fear*?

I have no idea.

It scares me every time.

The difference is, where I used to *avoid* public speaking because it made me nervous, now I just *do it*. I know I'll be nervous, but I *confront* it.

I do it anyway.

When I used to avoid public speaking I always felt cowardly about it, weak. When I get nervous and do it anyway, I come away feeling good about myself, and no one even knows how scared I was!

Anxiety is a normal human emotion. It's what we feel when we apply for a job we want; when we date someone who we like; when we do something that's important to us that we don't want to mess up.

When I tell people I have a fear of public speaking, they think I'm joking. People see me as a happy, charming, relaxed, talkative extrovert. The truth is I still get quite nervous about every talk and every performance I give.

How do you do it *without fear*?

I have no idea.

Just accept that you're going to be nervous, and do it because it's important to you.

Q. What gift can I buy my girlfriend who is a perfectionist who likes to have everything aligned and organized?

A. Therapy.

Q. Is humor ever used by therapists with their clients?

A. No. Not ever. In fact, we can lose our license for simply cracking a joke! One good friend of mine is serving time in prison for making a knock-knock joke with a client who had a phobia of wood!

Oops! I meant absolutely! Trust and connection are vital to being able to influence a client to change. You don't achieve that by playing "Dr. Aloof" or "Dr. Clearly-Smarter-Than-You." You achieve that by being human and approachable and making your clients comfortable. We deal with some serious topics and some fairly rigid clients in the therapy office. Humor helps a great deal.

Q. Do you recommend journaling to your clients?

A. I recommend journaling to my clients who enjoy writing. For those who do, I suggest keeping *two* journals: a positive and a negative journal. Write positive feelings, thoughts, and experiences in a permanent book because those entries will turn your mood around and make you feel great even 20 years from now.

Write the sad, fearful, and angry entries in your negative journal. That one should be a loose leaf book because once you get all those bad feelings out, the entry has no more value. It'll turn your mood around and make you feel like crap 20 years from now. When you finish writing an entry, tear those pages out, rip them into tiny pieces, and toss them away.

Q. How can I make an "off switch" for my thoughts?

A. Dr. Fritz Perls was fond of saying, "Lose your mind and come to your senses!"

Depressed people live in their heads. Anxious people live in their heads. People escape to their heads to avoid their feelings. Your head is a calculator. Its most useful purpose is to solve actual problems.

Life is out here, in the present moment.

Meditation can help because it trains you to focus. You become less distractable. Activities like dancing, playing a musical instrument, sports, dancing, or arts and crafts can help if they force you out of your head and into the moment.

It can also help to learn to tell yourself SHUT UP!!! Stamp your feet. Take some breaths. That snap-the-rubber-band-on-your-wrist trick works for some people, anything to get you grounded back in the *real* world.

Q. Is it true that the first two years of therapy are the hardest?

A. The first two out of *how many?*

Whenever I hear clients or colleagues talk about therapy in terms of years, my first thought is either the client isn't doing what he is told, or the therapist has no idea how to treat this client and is seeing him weekly anyway.

As for "years of therapy," I fault irresponsible therapists for this as much as unmotivated clients. I may work a few years with a rape victim or a schizophrenic, but the majority of my cases take weeks or months, not years. If a clinician doesn't know how to fix the problem or is unable to influence and motivate the client, they shouldn't just make chit-chat for years. That's not therapy. That's being a paid friend!

There is nothing I know that would take me *years* to teach! If I'm not teaching my clients to cope with their stressors without my help, then I'm not doing my job.

Someone told me that, because a relative recently died, she would have to see her therapist because, for the past 15 years, she always got her through the deaths of family and friends or any stressful situations. Lucrative as it may be, I don't want my clients to be dependent on me. I want to teach them what they need to know to live effectively *without* me.

Sometimes clients aren't emotionally ready to change the way they do things. That's understandable.

Therapists are like lawyers and mechanics. Just because we have the title and a license, doesn't mean we're very good at our job.

Q. I've been diagnosed with PTSD, and have made tons of progress dealing with it, but there is one aspect of the incest that I'm struggling to remember. What can you suggest?

A. My job is to help clients regain their *functioning*. We can hypnotize clients to recover memories, but it's reckless. If you don't remember something, it's probably because a part of you can't handle the memory. And that's okay.

I once worked with a 75-year-old Korean War veteran. He was emotionally stable and healthy after he returned from the Korean War. He had a wife, three children, a job. Then, decades later, he saw the movie, "Saving Private Ryan."

He left the theater with full-blown PTSD: a rageful temper, relationship difficulties, trust issues, hypervigilance, flashbacks – all because a Hollywood movie revived memories that had been dormant for 40 years. A part of his brain had closed down in Korea so that he could emotionally survive the horror of a sniper attack that killed most of his company. Then his memory shut down so that he could enjoy his life and family at home. What a shame that an $8 movie ruined that. The VA's position regarding "Saving Private Ryan" was, "If you were ever a combat veteran, skip this movie. If you never served in combat, don't miss it."

When my clients have a hole in their memory, I don't go chasing it down. How they function in their lives is all that matters.

Q. What kinds of successful outcomes have people achieved in therapy?

A. The best way I can sum up successful psychotherapy outcomes is by saying that people gain *choices* they didn't have before.

The woman who doesn't shop or eat at restaurants because she has agoraphobia, the guy whose fear of flying keeps him from traveling, the rape victim who can no longer be intimate with her husband, the combat veteran who can't hold a job due to his temper, the alcoholic who can't go a day without drinking, the 30-year-old who is too shy to ask a girl out ... They have all lost choices, so their lives are limited.

When psychotherapy is successful, people always gain choices.

Q. How can we tell the meaning of our dreams?

A. One of the few things that are factual about our dreams is the emotions they provoke. Often, this happens because we are repressing certain emotions during our waking hours. It has to come out somehow if we're to maintain our emotional equilibrium.

When we dream, our subconscious mind creates these little movies calculated to evoke specific emotions. The situation is often random, as are the characters in the dream.

I'll give you an hypothetical example: My boss barges into the office when I'm with a customer and yells at me. I can't yell back or punch his face because he's my boss and I need the job.

When I get home, I don't share this bad experience with my wife, because I'm not the type who shares my feelings. I'd rather watch TV, drink beer, and pass some gas. But that night I have a dream where I single-handedly slay an evil dragon with my mighty sword of justice!

What do you suppose *that* dream was about?

I once had a client show up for his appointment quite upset.

Rick: "What's wrong? You look upset."

Client: "I had this awful dream last night! I dreamed I was in bed having sex with *my mother*! And I was really into it! It was awful! I don't have any feelings like that for my mother! What in the hell was *that* supposed to mean??"

Rick: "It means you're horny. I'm sorry that your mom got cast in the role, but the casting was meaningless to your unconscious mind. Be happy you weren't in bed with your *father!*"

Forget the dream interpretation books. Anytime you want to know what your dream meant, ask yourself what feelings it provoked. Then ask yourself what is going on in your life that might cause those sorts of feelings. Score extra points if it's something you've been trying not to think about.

Q. Is it ethical to treat a patient that you sincerely dislike? What if another therapist is available? Should the patient be referred to the other therapist, or does it matter if you continue to treat them?

A. I can't address the ethics, but the few times I have done an intake on someone I disliked, I told the client that I was booked and had no room in my caseload, and transferred that client to another clinician for treatment.

When I was still a new dad and my son was only a year-old, I did an intake on a guy who had just been released from prison for molesting a six-year-old-boy. During the intake, he admitted to having done this to four other boys earlier (for which he never was caught.) There was no way I wanted to work with this guy, or even see him once a week! I was not the best therapist for him for two reasons: I wasn't trained to work with child molesters, and I didn't like the guy! He was transferred to a clinician down the hall who had no children.

Q. How do I know if I'm an Empath?
A. I am *so* the wrong person to ask this of since that term has been a pet peeve of mine for years.

First, some history: During the late 1980's, while writing his Star Trek series sequel, "Star Trek: The Next Generation," Gene Roddenberry invented the character Deanna Troi, a half-human, half-Betazoid from the planet Betazed. While pure Betazoids have telepathic ability, Deanna's half-human side caused her to be merely an "empath", which Roddenberry defined as a hyper-ability to sense emotions in others.

Before anyone gets their feathers ruffled, here is the Oxford Dictionary definition of "empath":

*"Pronunciation: /'empaTH/ **Definition of empath in English:** noun. (Chiefly in science fiction) a person with the paranormal ability to apprehend the mental or emotional state of another."*

Notice the distinction, "Chiefly in science fiction".

Now let's talk reality. Empathy is a human quality that was **not** manufactured by a science fiction writer. Like most human qualities, we have it in varying degrees. Some people are very empathetic, and some are not very empathetic, and most of us fall on a scale somewhere in between. And we jump around on that scale since we care about some people more than others.

An "empath" is not a separate classification of human being. That's ridiculous. At what point is a person so generous that he/she becomes a "*Generoso*"? Do we call a person with chronic gas a "*Flatuoso*"? Somewhere along the line, a new-agey person took Gene Roddenberry's word, "Empath" and began using it as if it meant something significant. Fortunately, they omitted its association with the planet Betazed!

Rather than saying that a person is very empathetic, they'll say that he or she is an "Empath." It's a silly label. At what point does an empathetic person *become* an empath? If that person meets someone she doesn't like and feels no empathy for, are they no longer an 'empath' from that day forward? Who decides? What measurement tools are available? Even Gene Roddenberry would have a laugh.

So, to answer your question, You are not an empath. You may be a particularly empathetic person. You may be very empathetic at times and less so, at other times, like most of our earth-bound species. Don't get too concerned over labels. They only exist to simplify what's complicated.

Aren't you glad you chose me to ask?

Live Long and Prosper.

Q. I want to be a therapist, but can't decide whether to follow the Psychology route or Sociology. Why did you choose to be licensed as a mental health counselor and not a social worker?
A. I can't answer that honestly without providing some personal context from my childhood.

When I was nine-years-old, my parents divorced. I wound up living with my mother. Smart as she was, she cleaned people's houses for $10 a day. My dad paid child support, but my mother got health insurance from the state welfare department. Because we were now considered to be on welfare, state social workers had the right to come into our apartment unannounced any time they pleased. This was during the 1960s and 1970s.

From age nine through 17, I grew up seeing random social workers barge into our home, asking my mother accusatory questions, often making her cry. They would search through our dresser drawers and our closets, hoping to find evidence of additional sources of income.

"Why does this boy own a typewriter?!" barked one social worker. "It is an old used one.", replied my mother. "It was a Christmas gift from his brother."

"Is this a *new* book? How did you afford to buy a book like this?", "Is that lamp new? It looks new.", "You can afford *canned salmon*?!"

We seldom saw the same social worker twice. A few of them were nice, respectful people, but most treated my mother as though she was a parasite.

Needless to say, I grew up with some negative feelings about social workers. When state welfare department budgets got slashed, many social workers began doing psychotherapy.

Later, the American Psychological Association decided that there should be masters-level clinicians trained in psychology, rather than sociology. The Licensed Mental Health Counselor was born.

Today's licensed social workers are often excellent clinicians. They use the same techniques open to any of us. Any modern social workers reading this will be as disgusted as anyone by the glimpse of what it was like to be "on welfare" in the 1960s.

Apart from the fact that I find sociology dull, compared with psychology, becoming a social worker had too many negative connotations for me. I became a licensed mental health counselor trained mostly by psychologists. The choice was personal.

Q. Is there any sort of work that would perpetually keep me happy? Is pain part of every profession?

A. Pain is a part of *everything*! The car you love will need repairs. The home you love will get a leaky roof or a broken faucet. At the job you love you'll answer to an incompetent manager. The love of your life will be a pain in the ass, from time to time.

It isn't our house, car, job or partner who makes us happy. We either learn to be happy people or we don't. "Happy" isn't a destination. It's a way of travel. Shit happens to happy people. Things break. We get robbed. Our jobs require we do things that make no sense. People we care about die. Happy people just get over it quicker. They perceive things in the best way possible.

Q. Why is depression so extremely common? I always hear: I'm so depressed; she's depressed; it's so depressing; I'm feeling depressed, etc... Almost everyone now suffers from this disease?

A. Bear in mind that lots of people substitute the word "depressed" when they mean "sad."

Depression is an emotional disease that has little to do with the events or situation in your life. Successful, happily-married, well-loved people can suffer from the disease of depression.

Sadness, on the other hand, is situational. "I'm *sad* because my brother died/my job sucks/I can't afford what I want/my friend hurt my feelings."

Lots of people think "depressed" means sad. It's why they tell depressed people to cheer up. They don't understand the mental illness called depression. They don't understand the feeling of not belonging. They can't relate to being completely unmotivated – lacking all enthusiasm – or feeling hopeless, helpless, and worthless. They don't understand the difficulty concentrating, constant fatigue, insomnia or hypersomnia, overeating or lack of appetite, or suicidal thoughts that often accompany depression. People who suffer from depression can seldom point to a specific reason. Sad and grieving people always can.

Q. But don't some people become depressed after losing a loved one?

A. We *grieve* the loss of a loved one. It is the normal, natural and healthy response to that loss. The grieving spouse is not suffering from a mental illness. The grieving spouse does not need an antidepressant or cognitive-behavioral therapy. We don't worry that the grieving spouse will commit suicide or wind up in a mental hospital.

In my entire career, I've worked with one person who suffered from major depression five years after the death of her son and one person who suffered from major depression six years after the death of his cat. Both clients suffered from dysthymic disorder *before* those deaths that became the focus of their major depression.

Q. Don't you think the Supreme Court's ruling in favor of same-sex marriage harms or diminishes currently recognized heterosexual marriage?

A. Do violently abusive heterosexual marriages diminish healthy marriages? Why should this?

In my practice, I've met married couples who cut and torture each other and consider it foreplay. Marriages where the husband farms his wife out to strangers for sex. Husbands who dress as sheep or sniff footwear. Wives who pee or poop on their husbands in the course of lovemaking.

Do you know what we call couples like these?

"Straight."

These are included in the marriages whose "sanctity" is supposedly threatened by gay marriage. We presume that all heterosexuals behave much like we do in the bedroom and that what gay people do is unnatural.

Take it from a "straight" therapist who knows better. If two people want to commit to one another for life, let them, and confine your interest to your own bedroom, lest you learn what the straight couple next door is doing.

Q. How do psychotherapists handle vicarious trauma?
A. I can't say I've ever experienced vicarious trauma. If I did, I'd talk with a fellow therapist.

One thing I *can* say I've observed is that war movies and rape scenes in movies have lost any entertainment value for me. I no longer see them as harmless, fake movie scenes. They remind me of real people who have been in those situations. I'm not *trauma-*

tized by them; I just don't enjoy those sorts of movies or scenes anymore.

Q. Should I become a therapist?

A. I'll tell you what I tell young people who are considering the mental health field: get in touch with The Samaritans and volunteer to man a helpline. You'll get free training from them, and the first time a stranger's life is in your hands, you'll know whether this is something that you love or hate.

Too many people have the impression that we just sit around empathizing with the "worried well", occasionally dishing out wise advice like enlightened gurus on mountaintops. The reality is considerably different, and it isn't for everyone. The reality includes schizophrenics and volatile people with hair-trigger tempers. The reality includes rape victims and women who were sexually abused in childhood. The reality includes people who threaten suicide for attention as well as people who sincerely want to be dead. If it's for you, by all means jump in! You're needed. My suggestion above is a good, free way to find out quicker and cheaper than a Master's degree, and you may help someone in the process!

I love doing psychotherapy. I love helping people get their lives and choices back as well as helping to save relationships. It's my contribution to this nutty world. Of course, not every client intervention is a success story, and you have to be okay with that, too.

Q. What is your opinion about biofeedback as a treatment for depression and anxiety?

A. There was some serious research done in England that showed light-sound machines and others to have some effectiveness in treating depression, anxiety, PMS and ADHD. There have been no such studies in the US because we invest all our hopes ($) and resources ($$) in the pharmaceutical industry ($$$).

I've worked with light-sound machines on myself. It's fascinating and powerful stuff! The first time a light-sound machine put me into the theta state, it scared the shit out of me! It was like tripping without drugs! Entraining brainwaves can put you to sleep (delta) or make you relaxed (alpha) or very alert (beta). The problem is you can't prescribe or expect a client to go out and buy a light-sound machine. I've used GSR biofeedback devices to train anxiety clients relaxation techniques. I'd love to work with EEG biofeedback, but it's fairly pricey to get into.

Q. What are the reasons for mental disorders? I know it's because of chemical imbalance, structural changes in the brain, but why does it happen?

A. "Chemical imbalance" is a term and concept introduced by the pharmaceutical industry. What better way to market chemical solutions than to say you're treating a chemical imbalance? The logic falls apart when you apply it to mental illness resulting from trauma or one's childhood.

Mental illness can be genetic, and it can be the result of an unstable or dysfunctional early home environment. We all experience varying amounts of stress throughout our lives, and we each have varying amounts of coping skills. When our stressors exceed our ability to cope with them, we experience mental illness.

Q. Should I be myself even if that means being brutally honest all the time?

A. No. Part of being mature is being discriminating and having a sense of judgment. I can walk up to a stranger and say, "Excuse me, but you are the ugliest person I've ever seen in my entire life!" and, while that may be *honest*, it's *unkind*, and kindness takes far more character and emotional maturity than brutal honesty.

Q. I know I have an anger issue, but I always apologize to my wife afterward. Do I still need to do something about the anger issue?

A. Only people who are close to me can hurt me with words said in anger. If they apologize, I'll forgive them, but every one of those reckless comments becomes a brick in an emotional wall between us that keeps me from being as open and trusting as I would prefer to be.

I recall a story about someone breaking a plate out of anger. Even after diligently gluing it back together, the plate would never be the same again. It works the same with our anger toward our loved ones.

Q. How can I fix my family?

A. Replace them.

I often say that we have two families: our "family of origin", that random group of people who we were thrust upon at birth (and who were thrust upon us) and our "adult family", the people we meet along the way who love us exactly the way we are and with whom we resonate. Our adult family is our intentional family, our family of choice, the people we chose and who chose us. Some of your original family members will become part of your adult family, but many may not.

I often see clients who as adults are still trying desperately to win the approval of their parents or siblings. I often think if they were incapable of treating you lovingly when you were young and cute and precious, why would they be different now? They did what they could based on what they learned, based on the quality of love that they received. If you managed to reach adulthood and your relationships with your parents or your siblings are not what you wish they were, find relationships elsewhere! That's what lovers and spouses and friends are for!

Friends are God's way of apologizing for our families.

What was missing from your childhood? Love? Humor? Fun? Closeness? Stability? Freedom? Intellectual stimulation? Expression of feelings? Approval?

Find *friends* who can supply those things.

I've met hundreds of people who were attracted to partners who possessed the same negative qualities as their worst parent: the woman with the alcoholic father who falls in love with and marries an alcoholic; the guy whose father was emotionally unavailable who marries an emotionally unavailable woman; the boy with the controlling mother who falls in love with one controlling girlfriend after another; the abused child who grows up and finds herself attracted to abusive men.

What were your parents' *positive* qualities? What positive qualities were missing? How about intentionally looking for those qualities in friends and partners instead of blindly stumbling toward what seems vaguely familiar?

I remember a woman telling me, "I'm jealous of my girlfriends. They all have great relationships with their sisters. They do cookouts together; they go on vacations together; they go shopping together. My sisters want nothing to do with me! We never do anything together."

I said, "Why not do those things with your friends? They already know how it's done. Suggest you all do a cookout, a movie or a shopping trip. Why would you want to do those things with women who would not choose to do them with *you*? Just because you're related? Do those things with the friends who love and value you!"

Not all of us were raised by perfect, emotionally stable and healthy families. Many of us were raised by dysfunctional families.

Live intentionally and consciously. Figure out what was lacking in your family of origin and get it from your adult family.

Q. Why do some people judge others without even knowing them?

A. When my son was much younger, he asked me my why racism existed. My answer was:

"Everyone needs to feel self-esteem. There are two ways of achieving self-esteem:

1) *Accomplish something or live a life that makes you feel good about yourself.*

2) *Tell yourself that you are, somehow, better than someone else.*

The fact is: #2 is easier."

Q. Why does my eight-month-old baby dislike me when I take him from his mother? He either turns his head or cries.

A. As the father of a grown son, the best book I ever read on parenting was *"Raising a Son"* by Don and Jeanne Elium. The first third of the book is a very insightful look at the masculine role in society and what goes wrong. The last 2/3 of the book addresses raising a boy, age by age.

The most helpful concept for me, when I was a new dad, was to learn that a boy bonded with his mom for the first 10 or 11 years of his life and that the most valuable thing a dad could do is to preserve and protect that relationship.

At around 10 or 11, the boy is ready to "cross the bridge" into manhood. It is now that mom becomes less cool. It is now that dad becomes the boy's primary focus, model, and teacher. Incidentally, if we do this right, we raise an adult man who has no qualms about being loving toward his mom again.

Q. What can a white psychologist or therapist do to build trust and rapport with clients who are not white?

A. I'm a white, heterosexual, Unitarian Universalist therapist who has worked successfully with Black, Asian, Hispanic, gay, lesbian, Catholic, Jewish, Protestant, and Muslim clients.

I do nothing, in particular, to build trust and rapport beyond being clear about who I am and being myself. As in any social situation, *if we pretend to be someone else we'll attract and repel the wrong people.*

A therapeutic relationship is like a friendship: You either "click" with a person or you don't. Some clients find my direct, blunt, confrontational, "let's-fix-what's-broken" style refreshing while others would consider me a nightmare. My only trick for building trust and rapport with *anyone* is to be my honest self.

Q. Why don't some men want children?

A. Because grown-up *women* are WAY more fun.

Q. Is hypnosis for real?

A. Lots of people have the wrong idea about hypnosis. The person doing the hypnosis does *not* have some weird control over you. We can't make you run naked in the street or rob a bank unless you're the type of person who enjoys running naked in the street or robbing banks.

Where I find hypnotherapy most helpful is when someone needs to do public speaking or get on a plane or through any anxiety-producing situation without drugs.

One of the important things to understand about hypnotherapy is that we can only get someone to do what they want. For example, no one *wants* to be nervous on a stage or a plane, so it's easy to get them to be calm via hypnosis.

On the other hand, telling a smoker she doesn't want a cigarette, or an overweight person he doesn't want to eat doesn't work out so well because, in fact, they *do* want to smoke or eat!

Lots of people swear by hypnosis as an effective way of quitting smoking. In actuality, that success rate is only 30%. But, that 30% is much more vocal about their success than the other 70% is about their failure. The 30% that succeeds was ready to quit before they were even hypnotized. If you gave them aspirin and told them it was a new "Quit Smoking Pill" it probably would have worked.

You can use hypnosis to recover lost memories but any information recovered is inadmissible in court since false info can be just as easily obtained if you ask leading questions.

Hypnotherapy works well with anxiety because no one *chooses* to over-react to anxiety. I like to give people a post-hypnotic "trigger" they can use on their own. For instance, "Anytime you squeeze your right knee with your left hand you'll begin to feel very calm and relaxed."

My favorite demonstration to prove that hypnosis works is to hypnotize someone and tell them that it's 120 degrees in the room and watch them perspire. You can't fake that.

Q. How much personal information should a therapist reveal to a client?

A. I'll share personal *experiences* with clients when I think it might help model a healthy approach to their problem. (e.g., marriage, parenting, personal growth, etc.)

Q. What is the most interesting mental illness and why?

A. Of the mental illnesses I've had direct experience with, I always found "*pica*" to be fascinating.

Pica sufferers have an appetite and a compulsion for eating non-edible things like pens, glass Christmas ornaments, the contents of ashtrays, paint, paper, wood, cleaning products, etc. In mental hospitals, drastic measures must be taken to keep common objects and substances away from patients who would eat them.

I remember one outpatient client telling me, "When I see Lestoil (a brand name of cleaning product) I have to open the bottle and *smell* it. Once I smell it, I have to *taste* it. Once I taste it, I have to *drink* a little. It makes me *sick*, but not enough to *kill* me."

That's pica.

Q. When you have worked so many years in the field, can new clients even surprise you anymore?

A. Oh yes! When new clients describe themselves as "abuse victims", we need more specific information. I've learned to ask clients for an example of the abuse at its worst. Imagine my surprise when a nurse from Georgia described her husband completely dousing her with gasoline when she was pregnant with their first daughter, then chasing her through their yard while tossing lit matches at her.

When interviewing alcoholics, it's common to meet someone who drinks a case of beer per day. (I couldn't drink a case of *water* per day!) But, I was sure surprised when I met a guy who admitted to drinking *two* cases of beer plus a pint of gin per day. His alcoholism was so severe; he could no longer ingest solid food.

It's routine to ask a new client's caffeine intake. One guy said he drank four 12-cup pots of coffee each day. I asked how he managed to fit that much coffee into his day. He said he drank a pot in the morning, one in the afternoon, and one in the evening. The fourth pot? He drank that overnight. He could only sleep for an hour or so. Then he would wake up and couldn't get back to sleep until he drank another cup of coffee. That allowed him to sleep for another hour or so. He was so addicted to caffeine he couldn't *sleep* without it!

People never stopped surprising me.

Q. Which behavior indicates happiness?

A. Resilience.

Too many people think of happiness as a destination, a plateau one reaches after years of climbing.

It's not.

Happiness is a way of travel. People who are "happy" are emotionally resilient. They experience the same tragedies, failures, and disappointments as anyone else, but they know in their heart that ultimately they'll survive any adversity (short of death), any loss, any disappointment that life sends their way.

I once had a client who felt my advice didn't apply to him because I was a "happy" person. I said, "Do you know what it's like to be happy? When everything is great at home, things probably suck at work. And when things are great at work, things probably suck at home. And on those occasions when things are going great at work *and* home, your car will probably die!"

I was being semi-facetious, but that *is* the way I see life. With humor and with the acceptance that bad stuff is going to happen and all I really can control is my attitude toward it and how I choose to react.

Three mistakes that people often make are letting their moods define them, letting other people define them, and letting their past define them.

Happy people understand that those who are critical of them are often revealing their *own* issues. They have self-esteem and self-respect and are quick to admit and forgive their mistakes. They are grateful for what they have. They appreciate and enjoy what is good in their lives. They recognize that the mind is for actual problem-solving, and don't use it to dwell in the past, obsess over the future, or avoid the present.

Happy people take responsibility for their mood. When they are tired of feeling sad or angry or scared or hopeless, they do whatever it takes to turn their mood around.

That's true happiness. It's a *choice* one makes.

"There is no path to happiness: happiness is the path."
~Gautama Buddha

SEMI-RETIREMENT

*"To know even one life has breathed easier because you have lived -
This is to have succeeded."* ~Bessie Anderson Stanley

Several years ago, when we still lived in Maine, when people
asked what I did for a living, I said I was a psychotherapist for
half the week and a drummer for the other half. The drumming
half of the week included drumming in a band, teaching group
drumming at a Waldorf high school, conducting workshops,
building drum mallets and beaters, and hosting a community
drum circle four times a month. Since moving to New Mexico, I
consider myself semi-retired. Now I just drum.

Two years ago, I received an email from a middle-aged Santa Fe
woman whose friends drummed in my community drum circle.
They told her that I was a drummer and a therapist and that I
seemed like a nice, approachable guy.

Her email explained that she had a stroke three years ago while
playing her drum. After spending a year recuperating, she found
she was afraid to even *look* at her drum again. She associated
drumming with her stroke. She wondered whether I would be
willing to see her as a therapy client.

In my email reply, I suggested that we meet for coffee first, and
she agreed. It was a Friday, and we decided that the following
Monday afternoon worked for both of us. In my next email, I
asked her to do me a favor that weekend.

"*Whichever room you're going to be in for any length of time, I want you to bring your drum in with you. Don't take it out of the case. Just put it in that room. When you're cooking, bring it in the kitchen. When you eat a meal or watch TV, bring your drum to that room. When you turn in for the night, put it in your bedroom. Don't look at your drum. Don't even open the case. Just put it in whatever room you're in. Don't play it. I just want it to be a familiar presence in the room with you. If that makes you unbearably nervous, put it away until you relax. Then bring it back out again, as many times as it takes. Just don't play it yet.*"

That Sunday evening, I received another email from her:

"*Okay Rick,*

So I received your email and got a bit teary with the thought of getting out my djembe. But I knew right away what I needed to do.

I asked my kind husband to stay by my side. I dusted off the djembe case, carried it outside onto the portal in the open air, sun and wind. I unzipped the case, eyes tearing up a bit and feeling a little shaky and took out the drum. It is a beautiful drum. I squatted down, hugged the drum in the warm sun and out came the words "You aren't the reason I had the stroke". I asked hubby to get a chair for me, put my knees around the drum and played for maybe a minute or so. I drummed on my djembe!!! It is so incredibly resonant even after three years of dormancy. I love my drum.

We went inside, had some tea, and I got teary again remembering the stroke and the aftermath, still a little shaky and my right arm got heavy, which relates to the moment of the stroke and after. Then I took a nap, feel better now and still emotional in a good kind of sentimental way.

So my djembe is still sitting out on the portal being purified by the elements. I will bring it in shortly, and it will live now, without the case, in our bedroom. I feel fearful of drumming on it in the house, and if I do so, it will be very softly. I won't play it much now, if at all. That big resonance frightens me for now. I am not as afraid of playing it loudly outdoors, at least, I don't think so. Thanks so much already Rick, and I haven't even met you in person yet. The positive process of letting go of my djembe fears has happily begun."

She and I met for coffee on Monday. We spent several hours chatting. She asked how much she owed me for helping her out. I said, "How can I charge you for an email? Consider it a 'drummer's discount.'" She insisted that she and her husband would like to take my wife and me out to dinner. I agreed. The four of us have been great friends ever since.

~:~:~:~:~:~

I'm still running a community drum circle, bringing people together who might otherwise have nothing much in common so that they can experience a few hours of mindfulness, recreational music-making, joy, and community. I still observe depressed people smiling and anxious people relaxing. I don't bill my drum circle as "therapeutic," but I promise you that there is some healing going on. I've drummed with at-risk youths, as well as a class-room of young, developmentally-delayed adults. I also drum in a blues band, two kirtan bands, and occasionally for belly dancers. I continue to build drum mallets and beaters and teach workshops, on occasion.

~:~:~:~:~

The chapter in this book on abusive relationships started out a few years ago as an online blog post. As a result, several dozen women found it and wrote me asking my opinions and advice re-garding their abusive situations. I helped as much as I could. I convinced half of them to leave and maintained online corre-spondences throughout the process. One 20-something-year-old Hindu woman in India calls me her "Angel Pa." A 31-year-old re-cently divorced Muslim woman living in the US calls me her "guardian angel" and insists that she won't even date anyone until the guy talks with me first.

Here is a message I received anonymously while writing this book. The writer is referring to the same online posting:

"Because of the knowledge you have armed me with, I want you to know you just may have saved my life. I have always known these things you spoke of for the most part, but since the abuse started, I have increasingly become unsure.... unsure of EVERYTHING I thought I knew. What you wrote has reassured me and am going to pack a suitcase (secretly) with my necessities as soon as I am fin-ished writing you. Since I am financially dependent on my abuser and am disabled, my escape plan will take some extensive plan-ning. But I would rather be broke, afraid and homeless than

DEAD. I can not express my gratitude enough. Your kindness and comforting wisdom may have saved my life. You are more important than you know."

~:~:~:~:~

During the first few months after moving to New Mexico while visiting the Santo Domingo Pueblo, I met a pueblo Indian named Robert, who made and sold jewelry. He also teaches native folklore and traditions. We talked about our move to Santa Fe and my drum circles and the differences between community drum circles and the sacred, ceremonial drumming of his culture. We had a nice time chatting. Before I left, he welcomed me to New Mexico, handed me a beaded bracelet, and told me to hang it somewhere in our house for luck.

No charge.

A year later, I brought my friend Muriel and her friend Karen to the Santo Domingo Pueblo so they could shop for jewelry. I spotted Robert. We had run into each other a few times over the past year, usually on pueblo feast days. We shook hands and chatted a while. I introduced him to our Massachusetts visitors.

As I was saying goodbye, he smiled and held his closed fist out to me as if about to hand me something quietly. I put out my hand, and he dropped a turquoise arrowhead into it. He said simply, "For protection." The arrowhead was carved from Kingman turquoise, of the now closed Kingman mine in Arizona, prized for its high quality and sky blue color.

Again, though he was there selling jewelry — no charge.

Last year, we had lunch at the home of an Acoma Indian family at the Acoma Pueblo on their feast day. My squash soup needed salt, so I asked our host for some. He handed me a salt shaker, and I shook some salt into my soup.

Our host said, "I had a choice of two salts to give you: the one from the store or the Indian salt. I gave you the Indian salt."

It turned out that "Indian salt" is from the Zuni Salt Lake. Acoma Indians make an annual 100+ mile pilgrimage to collect this salt. It is considered sacred. There is a fascinating legend involving "Mother Salt" of the Zuni Salt Lake. Look it up sometime. Five of the 19 pueblos, including Acoma, consider this salt sacred and make pilgrimages to collect it.

...and I sprinkled it in my soup!

(I know that I've buried the lead... But I'm getting to it.)

Before moving to New Mexico in 2013, most of my friends know that my bicep muscle was torn from inside my elbow while lifting a heavy box. It required emergency surgery and a two-month break from lifting or drumming. Dozens of drum circle folks came to the rescue, helping me pack and move boxes in preparation for our move.

My friend, Mary, had an idea. She gathered a bunch of friends to-gether to give me a group Reiki healing session. I lay there sur-rounded by these wonderful souls performing Reiki on me. They did this on two separate days, in fact. One woman, Patricia, even knitted me a "healing scarf" which I wore during the session and own to this day. She made it by saying prayers for healing with each stitch.

I could tell you dozens more stories like this. What's my point?

Do I believe that a beaded bracelet will bring luck? Or that a turquoise arrowhead will give me "protection"? Do I believe in the spiritual and healing properties of Indian salt from the Zuni Salt Lake? Or group Reiki? Or a Healing Scarf? Do I believe that people "drumming healing energy" for me actually heals me? When I drummed "healing energy" for my friend George during his foot surgery, do I believe that my drumming led to the posi-tive outcome?

No. Not really.

While I consider myself open-minded, I'm also fairly concrete.

Do you know what I **do** believe in?

LOVE... and caring.

The jeweler who gave me a $340 Navajo ring last year as a gift, the woman who anonymously paid for the church space for our Maine drum circle reunion, our friend who, while visiting Santa Fe, bought us a sterling silver Kokopelli riding a motorcycle... all surprising acts of kindness, caring, and love.

All report cards from God. (...or the Universe or Spirit)

That turquoise arrowhead says, "I care about you and want you to be safe and well." It says this in the language of an ancient culture and tradition, but I understand the language perfectly.

My squash soup would have tasted as good with the store-bought salt. Handing me the sacred Indian Salt instead spoke volumes, which had nothing to do with salting my soup.

Every one of the people who participated in the group Reiki could have gone home and had supper after a long day of work. Instead, they showed up to help me heal.

Did it work? Well, the surgeon told me my arm *might* be ready for drumming by mid-August. I drummed in a local parade on July 19; on stage with the Different Drummers Band on July 20, and then on stage with Bluezberry Jam on July 21. And I've been drumming ever since! My arm is good as new.

I think it's love and caring that works the magic.

I'm not saying that everything else is bullshit. We will never fully comprehend without a doubt exactly how this universe works. Everything is projection. We each create and respond to our own interpretation of what we perceive based on what we believe. I'm just saying that, in my perception, the common denominator is love and caring.

Sometimes I wonder if all the fancy techniques in my psychotherapy "toolkit" are what works the magic with clients or that I sincerely care about their mental health and the choices they make.

Have I been handing out turquoise arrowheads without even realizing it?

I sincerely hope so.

That's the guy I want to be.

~:~:~:~:~

This is what my "semi-retirement" looks like. It remains a privilege to help people, whether online or in person, simply because I can. Anything I have ever done for others has been returned in one form or another. My depressed teen-self who was so sure that this world would be a better place without him has been humbled more times than I can count.

If life was a ride, I'd go again.

Closing Parable

(Author unknown)

A traveler came upon an old farmer hoeing in his field beside the road. Eager to rest his feet, the traveler hailed the farmer, who seemed happy enough to stop and chat.

"What sort of people live in the next town?" asked the stranger.

"What were the people like where you've come from?" replied the farmer, answering the question with another question.

"They were a bad lot, troublemakers all, and lazy too. They were the most selfish people in the world, and not a one of them could be trusted. I'm happy to be leaving the scoundrels."

"Is that so?" replied the old farmer. "Well, I'm afraid that you'll find the same sort in the next town."

Disappointed, the traveler trudged on his way, and the farmer returned to his work.

Some time later another stranger, coming from the same direction, hailed the farmer, and asked, "Can you tell me what sort of people live in the next town?"

"What were the people like in the last town you visited?"

"They were the best people in the world, hard working, honest, and friendly. I'm sorry to be leaving them."

"Fear not," said the farmer. "You'll find the same sort in the next town."

Acknowledgments

I would like to take this opportunity to thank my friend, Ed Rooney, who generously helped edit this book. This is the third book of mine that Ed has read and edited before it saw print. This one was as difficult to edit as it was to write. Ed knows my writer's voice. He doesn't try to make me sound like everyone else. Ed made sure that my message was clear, flowing, and logical. He told me when the reader needed more details.

I also owe a debt of gratitude to my friend, Gloria Pendlay, who put as much time and effort into editing this book as anyone. I thought I had a pretty good handle on grammar before Gloria took her red pen to this book. If you should spot any grammatical errors, they are probably there because I insisted on them, not because Gloria missed them.

I would also like to thank Molly Person McNeece, my cover illustrator. It was her idea to portray one nut helping other nuts out of the can. For that stroke of brilliance, I'll be forever grateful.

I would like to thank my "test readers," who read this book before it was ready for publication and shared their valued opinions and suggestions. They were Mary Cote-Diaz, Marcia Putnam, Edmund Charles Davis-Quinn, and Joel Gendler.

Lastly, I'd like to dedicate this book to my beautiful wife and best friend, Judy. After 32 years of marriage, I consider myself lucky to look forward to the *next* 32 years.

55320659R00181

Made in the USA
Charleston, SC
25 April 2016